Now Playing

Learning Mythology through Film

Instructor's Edition

Gail Rosen
Eva M. Thury
Margaret K. Devinney

New York   Oxford
Oxford University Press

Oxford University Press, Inc., publishes works that further Oxford University s
objective of excellence in research, scholarship, and education.

Oxford New York
Auckland Cape Town Dar es Salaam Hong Kong Karachi
Kuala Lumpur Madrid Melbourne Mexico City Nairobi
New Delhi Shanghai Taipei Toronto

With offices in
Argentina Austria Brazil Chile Czech Republic France Greece
Guatemala Hungary Italy Japan Poland Portugal Singapore
South Korea Switzerland Thailand Turkey Ukraine Vietnam

For titles covered by Section 112 of the U.S. Higher
Education Opportunity Act, please visit
www.oup.com/us/he for the latest information about
pricing and alternate formats.

Published by Oxford University Press, Inc.
198 Madison Avenue, New York, New York 10016
http://www.oup.com

ISBN: 978-0-19-992939-9

Printing number: 9 8 7 6 5 4 3 2 1

Printed in the United States of America
on acid-free paper

CONTENTS

Introduction

Films provide much more than entertainment. They often reflect the values, beliefs, and concerns of their audience, and can provide valuable insights to students of mythology. They can also be used to enhance students' understanding of challenging subject matter, facilitate class discussion, and foster an energetic and exciting atmosphere in the classroom. This film supplement, new to the third edition, covers 30 films and three episodes from contemporary television series. Each entry in the supplement contains references to specific chapters in *Introduction to Mythology, Third Edition,* to enable smooth integration of the supplement with the fascinating and wide-ranging ideas in the book.

The information in the supplement facilitates discussion about either an entire film or one or more short scenes in a film. Each entry includes recommended clips with a time and minute counter. These clips can stand alone or be used in combination, if viewing the entire film is not practical. Data about producers, directors, and actors are included in each entry. This will enable students and instructors to locate the films, as well as criticism about them. The supplement also provides background information as well as a synopsis. This will allows instructors and students unfamiliar with the film to make an informed decision about which films to use. This will also help to compare and contrast the different versions of stories that evolve from the myths as well as identify central ideas within them. Each entry also includes questions that can start a class discussion or inspire written assignments. Suggested answers are provided in the Instructor's version. These answers emphasize important elements of each film and suggest connections to the material in *Introduction to Mythology.*

The films discussed in the supplement are from time periods ranging from 1948 to 2011. Included are films from places such as Indonesia, Brazil, and others, as well as the United States. The films used are critically acclaimed, animated, musicals, and big-budget adventures as well as low-budget gems. Some tell familiar stories in new ways, some explore mythological concepts in surprising ways, and some combine contemporary stories with ancient traditions. Some of these films reached a wide audience, while others may be unfamiliar to many. All contain moments of beauty, and all teach something useful about mythology and provide new and different perspectives on fascinating material.

It is hoped that this supplement will be useful and enjoyable, and will enable the discovery of new and exciting films and the rediscovery of familiar favorites.

1. *Beauty and the Beast (La belle et la bête)*

Film Data

Year: 1946

Director: Jean Cocteau

Length: 96 minutes

Rated: N/A

Characters/Actors

Jean Marais:	La Bête (The Beast)/The Prince/Avenant
Josette Day:	Belle
Mila Parély:	Félicie
Nane Germon:	Adélaïde
Michel Auclair:	Ludovic
Raoul Marco:	The Usurer
Marcel André:	Belle's Father

Connection to Chapters

Chapter 34. Applying Theory: How to Perform a Jungian Analysis

Chapter 37. Germany: Grimms' *Household Tales*

Recommended Scenes

The scene of the introduction with the text occurs at 00:02:32 through 00:03:35.

The scene of Belle's father entering the castle and making the deal with the Beast occurs at 00:17:05 through 00:24:55.

The scene of Belle's initial encounter with the beast occurs at 00:36:20 through 00:40:30.

The scene of the Beast drinking from Belle's hands occurs at 00:49:50.

The scene of the Beast asking Belle's forgiveness occurs at 00:54:47.

The scene of Belle attempting to give her sisters jewels occurs at 01:06:48.

The scene of Belle's love saving the beast and the resolution of the story occurs at 01:25:15.

Instructor Viewing Information

The French film (with English subtitles) *Beauty and the Beast* is the work of acclaimed filmmaker Jean Cocteau. Students may be unfamiliar with Cocteau and may require a bit of introduction and context to fully appreciate the film. *Beauty and the Beast* is loosely based on a tale by Jeanne-Marie Leprince de Beaumont, although students may recognize some elements from both household tales the *Beauty and the Beast and Cinderella*. Although this black-and-white 1946 film does not have the benefit of contemporary digital effects, students should enjoy the clever effects and serious filmmaking. This film was made for adults, and differs from the more contemporary children's films of this tale. *Beauty and the Beast* will provide an excellent way to discuss the layers of meaning in the household tales, as well as Jung's and Rank's ideas pertaining to household tales.

Synopsis

Lovely Belle (Day) is treated like a servant by her two mean sisters, who believe they are too beautiful to work. When Avenant (Marais) proposes to Belle, she refuses because she wants to stay with her debt-ridden father. After failing to resolve his financial affairs, Belle's father (André) gets lost in the forest and finds himself in a creepy castle. He takes a rose for Belle and incurs the wrath of the Beast (Marais). The Beast says he will kill him unless one of his daughters agrees to die in his place. When Belle learns of this, she sneaks away to the Beast's castle in order to save her father's life. But the Beast treats Belle very well and dines with her at seven o'clock each night. Each night he proposes marriage and Belle refuses. Belle finds the Beast repulsive, but sees he has a good heart. The Beast allows Belle to visit her ailing father and she promises to return within a week. Belle heals her father when she returns home. But Belle's sisters are jealous of Belle because of the riches the Beast bestowed on Belle. They trick Belle into staying with them and plan to steal the Beast's riches. They convince Avenant and their bother Ludovic (Auclair) to rescue Belle and help steal the Beast's treasures. When Belle realizes the Beast is dying, she returns to him. Avenant is shot and turns into a beast, and the Beast transforms into a handsome man who looks like Avenant. The former Beast says he was saved by a loving look from Belle. She also loves him, and becomes his Queen. The film ends as they happily float away.

Discussion Questions

1. **Explain how the film reflects the values and ethics of the time period when it was made.**

   This film was made right after World War II and the Nazi occupation of France. The future of the French film industry was in doubt, and many people thought *Beauty and the Beast* would be an important film. As horrors of World War II were still fresh, politics and evil were very much on the minds of the most people. The film starts with the credits on a blackboard and some text explaining the story. The text explains that the story involves a beast whose hands smoke when he slays a human victim. This may have special meaning for those familiar with the evils perpetuated during this time period. The text also asks the viewer to look at the film the way children look at things. Cocteau may have been directing this to critics of his work, who believed that an artist should be politically committed. He may have wanted to make his point that the childlike quality of the artist is most important, even more important than political commitment.

2. **Describe the ways that the film, like the stories of the Grimm Brothers, is directed primarily at adults.**

   The beginning of the film includes credits on a chalkboard and a written introduction to the story. Most of the story is told in this introduction, so the filmmaker assumed that the story was probably known to adults. The introduction is about childhood, rather than for children. The film also deals with the adult themes of duality and desire. Belle is both repulsed by and attracted to the Beast. She tells him that he had a good heart, but he is also a monster. But she also points out that there are bad people in the world who conceal their evil. She repeatedly refuses his offer of marriage, yet she enjoys spending time with him. She allows him to drink water from her hands in a sensual manner. The Beast appears at Belle's door covered with blood and she sees his hands smoking. He asks forgiveness for being a beast, and Belle tells him that he should be ashamed. It appears he has given in to his nature and killed someone, yet Belle still cares for him. At the end of the film, the Beast laments his nature, but Belle still declares her love for him. When Belle realizes that the Beast may die because she delayed returning to him, she declares that she is the monster. When the Beast is finally transformed into a handsome prince, Belle seems almost disappointed. She jokes about having to get used to his new appearance, but we sense she may miss the Beast.

3. Describe how the film portrays traditional values.

Unlike her selfish sisters Félicie (Parély) and Adélaïde (Germon), Belle is devoted to her father. When he first journeys from his home, the materialistic sisters ask their father for worldly goods, while Belle requests a simple rose. Although the sisters try to blame Belle for their father's punishment for stealing the rose, it is clear that selfishness is linked with desire for material possessions. Belle, who wanted a rose, volunteers to save her father's life by taking his place. But although Belle is willing to trade her life for her father's life, the moment the Beast sees Belle he tells her that she is not in danger and treats her with kindness and respect. The implication may be that her goodness is rewarded or that the Beast assumes that any daughter who would volunteer to trade her life for her father's must be a good person. The Beast shows this by showering Belle with fine clothes and jewels and proposing marriage to her. Belle's disregard for material possessions is thought to be a good quality, and she is rewarded with riches. When Belle returns home, she attempts to give her jewels to her envious sisters. But when the sisters touch the jewels, they are transformed into ugly items. Again, Belle is rewarded for her goodness, and her sisters are punished for their evil ways. At the end of the film, Belle is rewarded with riches and a happy life with a handsome prince. When the Beast transforms into a handsome man, he tells Belle that he was saved by a loving look. In this film, love and goodness can transform a beast into a man.

2. Black Orpheus (Orfeu Negro)

Film Data

Year: 1959

Director: Marcel Camus

Length: 100 minutes

Rated: PG

Characters/Actors

Breno Mello:	Orfeo
Marpessa Dawn:	Eurydice
Marcel Camus:	Ernesto
Fausto Guerzoni:	Fausto
Lourdes de Oliveira:	Mira
Léa Garcia:	Serafina
Ademar Da Silva:	Death
Alexandro Constantino:	Hermes

Connection to Chapters

Chapter 44. Poetry and Myth

Recommended Scenes

The scene of Mira saying she is not interested in old stories occurs at 00:014:45.

The scene of Orpheus meeting Eurydice occurs at 00:29:00 through 00:32:45.

The scene of Orpheus and Eurydice fighting and stopping death occurs at 00:47:34.

The scene of Eurydice's death occurs at 01:20:50.

The scene of Orpheus searching for Eurydice at the hospital and the police station occurs at 01:24:14 through 01:28:58.

The scene of Orpheus and the janitor who helps him occurs at 01:30:10 through 01:32:10.

The scene of Orpheus contacting Eurydice at the ceremony occurs at 01:36:36 through 01:38:51.

Instructor Viewing Information

Black Orpheus is in Portuguese with English subtitles. It won an Academy Award in 1960. The film contains long dance sequences without dialogue, and students may find it a bit slow-moving. The film may require some introduction and context. *Black Orpheus* features the wonderful music of acclaimed musician Antonio Carlos Jobim. The film provides a nice way to discuss the ways myths are adapted to reflect the concerns of audiences of varying places and time periods.

Synopsis

This modern interpretation of the myth of Orpheus and Eurydice is set in Rio de Janeiro, days before Carnival. It features a mostly black cast. Orpheus (Mello) is a streetcar conductor and a musician. His guitar playing and singing are said to make the sun rise. Orpheus is engaged to mean and controlling Mira (Oliveira), but he seems reluctant to marry her and continues to flirt with other women. This changes when Orpheus quickly falls in love with Eurydice (Dawn), a shy girl visiting her cousin Serafina (Garcia). Eurydice says she is being chased by a man who is trying to kill her. As the characters dance at Carnival, a masked and costumed figure that looks like Death (Da Silva) chases Eurydice. Orpheus tries to rescue her, but Eurydice is electrocuted on a wire while Death looks on. Orpheus refuses to believe that Eurydice is dead. He searches for her in a hospital and police station, and is finally directed to the missing persons department. There, Orpheus meets a janitor who takes him to a place guarded by a barking dog named Cerberus. Orpheus participates in a ceremony to contact the dead and hears the voice of Eurydice. She tells him he can only hear her if he does not look back. He does look back and she tells him she will be lost to him forever. Orpheus retrieves Eurydice's body from the morgue and lovingly carries her to a hill. A stone thrown by an angry Mira hits him, and Orpheus and Eurydice fall from the hill. The film ends with the little boys who have been following Orpheus throughout the film playing Orpheus' guitar and singing. A little girl joins them and dances, as they make the sun rise.

1. **Explain how the film uses the myth to reflect the current concerns of its time and place.**

   Black Orpheus focuses on the plight of poor blacks living in Rio de Janeiro. In 1959 when the film was released, issues of race and class would have been especially resonant. In this film, Orpheus works as a conductor on a streetcar. Eurydice is a farm girl who is visiting the city. All of the characters live in slum dwellings that may not have indoor plumbing. Orpheus shares his hovel with chickens and other animals. The girls in the town rarely have cash, and trade kisses for food with a lascivious merchant. But in the midst of poverty, the characters eagerly prepare for Carnival. They wear colorful and elaborate costumes and rehearse dance numbers. In the slum, Orpheus is a bit of a star, known for his musical abilities and dance routines. The splendor and excitement of Carnival works well in conjunction with the myth. The dancing, the beat of the music, and the costumes suggest another world, a place where identities are changed or concealed. The characters are poor, but they attempt to live their lives with joy and dignity, even though their hillside dwellings overlook a sprawling and wealthy city. When Eurydice is killed, Orpheus looks for her in a crowded hospital, where the employees seem overworked and unwilling to help him. At the police station, an officer recognizes Orpheus and asks him to sing and dance. When Orpheus explains that he is looking for Eurydice, the officer reluctantly points him to the missing persons office and still requests that Orpheus perform. In both places, Orpheus is treated as a second-class citizen. The janitor who offers to help Orpheus is the only person he encounters who treats him with compassion.

2. **Describe how the film interprets the myth to reflect the changing tastes and expectations of its audience.**

   In this film, there are no gods present, nor is there an underworld in the traditional sense. The film suggests that perhaps the hospital and police station are a kind of Hell. When Orpheus reaches the missing persons office, he finds a room filled with papers, but no people. Orpheus then descends a long and winding staircase with the janitor who acts as his guide. His search for Eurydice takes him to a native ceremony in which a woman tries to contact the dead. The characters do not seem to believe in fate, but fate seems inescapable for these characters. When Orpheus and Mira try to obtain a wedding license, the clerk asks Mira if her name is Eurydice. Mira says that she is not interested in old stories, but it is clear that Orpheus and Eurydice are destined to be together. When Orpheus stops Death from taking Eurydice, Death tells him they will meet again soon. Despite what the characters may want, Death soon claims Eurydice. The film also shows characters that are openly sexual, as an audience at that time may have expected. Serafina and her boyfriend are bawdy, and their sexual behavior is used as comic relief. Music is also an integral part of *Black Orpheus*. Here, Orpheus is a great musician, but he plays contemporary music on his guitar. The film features exciting and vibrant bossa nova and samba music that is very important to Brazil, and became even more popular after the film was released.

3. *Buffy the Vampire Slayer,* "The Gift"

Film Data

Year: 2001, Season 5, episode 22

Director: Joss Whedon

Length: 44 minutes

Rated: TV/PG

Characters/Actors

Sarah Michelle Gellar:	Buffy Summers
Nicholas Brendon:	Xander Harris
Alyson Hannigan:	Willow Rosenberg
Emma Caulfield:	Anya
Michelle Trachtenberg:	Dawn Summers
James Marsters:	Spike
Anthony Head:	Rupert Giles
Clare Kramer:	Glory
Charlie Weber:	Ben

Connection to Chapters

Chapter 15. Theory: Joseph Campbell, *The Hero with a Thousand Faces* (Dave Whomsley)

Chapter 39. Applying Theory: Highlighting Different Aspects of the Same Tale Using Multiple Analyses

Chapter 43. The Vampire as Hero: Tales of the Undead in a Contemporary Context

Recommended Scenes

The opening scene of Buffy killing a vampire occurs at the start of the episode through 00:02:34.

The scene of Anya giving Buffy the magical hammer occurs at 00:08:57.

The scene of Giles explaining the ritual to Buffy occurs at 00:11:51 through 00:12:19.

The scene of Glory explaining the ritual to Dawn occurs at 00:27:00.

The scene of Buffy telling Giles she will not kill Dawn occurs at 00:13:40 through 00:15:22.

The scene of Buffy sparing Ben and Giles killing Ben occurs at 00:36:01 through 00:37:41.

The scene of Buffy sacrificing herself by jumping off the tower occurs at 00:37:55 through the end of the episode.

Instructor Viewing Information

The premise of *Buffy the Vampire Slayer* is that in every generation, one girl is chosen to fight the vampires and evil in the world. That girl is helped by an adult who is called the Watcher. Buffy (Gellar) is the chosen girl, and Giles (Head) is her watcher. Buffy is also helped by a group of friends. Many students will have some familiarity with the series *Buffy the Vampire Slayer* and the characters. But even those who are unfamiliar with the series will enjoy and appreciate *Buffy the Vampire Slayer,* "The Gift." Students will enjoy the humor and action sequences in this episode. "The Gift" should provide a good starting point for a discussion of multiple perspectives and insights for a contemporary story. The episode also provides an excellent way to attempt to apply Joseph Campbell's ideas about the hero's journey to a female hero and Melanie Klein's ideas about mothering and females in vampire stories.

Synopsis

In Season 5 of *Buffy the Vampire Slayer,* Buffy must battle Glory (Kramer), a fallen god, who shares a body with a human doctor, Ben (Weber). In "The Gift," the Season 5 finale, Glory has taken Buffy's sister, Dawn (Trachtenberg). Dawn was created with mystical energy, and her blood, when used in a specific ritual, will open the door between dimensions. The evil Glory wants to perform this ritual and bleed Dawn, so Glory can return to another evil dimension and once again become a god. Buffy learns that if the ritual is started, the only way to stop it and save humanity will be to kill Dawn. Buffy tells Giles and her friends that she will not kill Dawn or let anyone else do so. Buffy, Willow (Hannigan), Xander (Brendon), Spike (Marsters), and Anya (Caulfield) work together to stop Glory. They defeat Glory, but the ritual has been started. Dawn offers to kill herself to stop the dimensions from bleeding together, but Buffy stops her. Buffy realizes that she can jump off the tower and stop the destruction and does so. Buffy sacrifices her life to save humanity.

Discussion Questions

1. **Explain how Buffy illustrates Campbell's idea of destiny calling a hero.**

    The episode begins with a scene that typifies the entire series. A vampire attacks a teenage boy and Buffy easily destroys the vampire and saves the boy. The shocked boy looks at Buffy and exclaims that Buffy is just a girl. "That is what I keep saying," answers Buffy. Buffy did not seek to be a hero, and resisted the call to adventure. She shows this by saying that she would rather be a regular girl than a hero. But as for Odysseus, the choice was made for Buffy. Destiny called Buffy; it was her fate to be the vampire slayer and thus a hero. Her "spiritual center of gravity" was transferred from the ordinary world she knew to the unknown world of supernatural evil. In the middle of the episode, Buffy tells Giles that if Dawn dies, she is finished with saving the world. But Buffy finds a way to follow her destiny, despite what she says. She continues being a hero and saves humanity by sacrificing her life. When Dawn tries to stop Buffy, Buffy insists, "This is the work that I have to do."

2. **Describe how Buffy takes the steps in the hero's journey as outlined by Campbell.**

    In synthesizing the ideas of both Otto Rank and Carl Jung, Campbell emphasized the importance of both male and female figures in the hero's adventure. Although Campbell's analysis envisioned a male hero, it is instructive to examine the way contemporary female hero figures may follow some of these same patterns. Campbell bases his ideas on a gendered, Freudian model: the male hero fights a (same-sex) father figure and resists a(n) (opposite-sex) temptress and unites with a(n) (opposite-sex) goddess. Here, however, the hero is female and these genders are for the most part reversed. Destiny has called Buffy to be a hero. By following her destiny to battle supernatural evil, Buffy enters a place that is unknown. In this episode Buffy must battle a god, an entity that she has not yet encountered; in accordance with the gender reversal of the hero tale, she undertakes "mother atonement": making Glory, the female villain, pay for her crimes. Buffy is, in effect, entering an unknown place in her world of unknown places. As she and her friends prepare for this battle and this adventure, Buffy receives supernatural, psychological, and physical help. Anya provides Buffy with a magical hammer that is considered to be a weapon of the gods. Much like Ben Kenobi in *Star Wars,* Giles is an older male and father figure who provides Buffy with advice. All of Buffy's friends assist her in battling Glory. Near the end of the episode, Buffy manages to trap Glory. Buffy is ready to kill the evil god when Glory changes into her human form, Ben. Buffy resists the temptation to kill Ben, even though it might be necessary in order to finally stop Glory. Her sense of morality will not allow her to kill another human being. After Buffy leaves, Giles tells Ben that Buffy cannot take a human life and is a hero, "not like us." Giles then kills Ben. This is similar to Ben Kenobi protecting Luke by cutting off an attacker's arm in the bar. Here Giles is protecting the world, Buffy, and Buffy's morality. Buffy saves Dawn's life and humanity by sacrificing herself and entering an unknown place for a new adventure. Before Buffy jumps to her death, she asks Dawn to tell Giles that she "has figured it out and I am okay." This suggests a new enlightenment and understanding of her human existence.

3. **Describe how the last scene in the episode illustrates Campbell's idea of crossing the threshold and the belly of the whale.**

Near the end of the episode, Buffy finds Dawn tied up on the highest tower in town. This is a good example of Buffy crossing a threshold. She sees the dimensions bleed together, and frightening mythological creatures are hurled from another world into her world. Buffy knows that she must enter this unknown place in order to complete the adventure. She makes a graceful leap from the tower into the mystical pool of energy. By then end of the episode, it appears Buffy is dead. But spiritually, she may be in the belly of the whale. She must possibly face unknown trials. At the start of the following season, Buffy is brought back to life. She has, in a way, been reborn. Buffy leaves a magical realm to return to an ordinary one, and continues to fight evil. She has also undertaken Campbell's idea of a spiritual quest. In the following season, Buffy achieves apotheosis. She has been changed by her "death" and comes to understand more about the spiritual side of human existence, while continuing to pursue her hero's quest.

4. **Explain how *Buffy the Vampire Slayer* shows Melanie Klein's ideas about "inappropriate mothering."**

Buffy had a close, but complicated, relationship with her mother throughout the series. Buffy's parents divorced when Buffy was young, and Buffy's father was not a presence in her life. In the fifth season of the series, Buffy encounters many changes. Buffy's mother dies, and Buffy feels like an orphan. As a college student who must now care for her younger sister Dawn, Buffy assumes a maternal role. This is a challenge for Buffy, as she has grown more aggressive in her pursuit of vampires and other evil forces. In this episode, Buffy is told that the only way to save the world is for Dawn to die. Buffy refuses to allow this, saying that she will protect Dawn even if means death for everyone. When Buffy explains her connection to Dawn, it is clear that she sees Dawn as her child rather than her sister. She explains that see feels that Dawn is part of her. As Buffy thinks about this impossible choice, she states, "I just wish my mom was here." Buffy now remembers her mother as the "good mother" who would know the right choice to make. In "The Gift," Glory represents the "bad mother." Glory is young, beautiful, and strong, like Buffy. But she is greedy and lusts for power, and will kill anyone who stands in her way. She intends to kill Dawn. Throughout the season and the episode, Buffy has struggled with her identity, wondering if her only purpose is to bring death. By the end of the episode she is able to come to terms with her dark or "bad" mother side, as well as her "good" mother side. Buffy finds a way to protect Dawn while still protecting the world. She combines her strength with her need to protect Dawn. Buffy sacrifices herself to save Dawn, but also to save the world.

4. *Clash of the Titans* (1981)

Film Data

Year: 1981

Director: Desmond Davis

Length: 118 minutes

Rated: PG

Characters/Actors

Zeus: Laurence Olivier

Hera: Claire Bloom

Thetis: Maggie Smith

Perseus: Harry Hamlin

Andromeda: Judi Bowker

Ammon: Burgess Meredith

Cassiopeia: Siân Phillips

Calibos: Neil McCarthy

Connection to Chapters

Chapter 1. What Is Myth?

Chapter 3. Greece: Hesiod

Chapter 4. Rome: Ovid

Chapter 32. Greece: Heracles and Dionysus

Recommended Scenes

The scene of Hera and Thetis discussing Zeus' womanizing occurs at 00:21:00.

The scene of Zeus and Thetis manipulating the clay models of humans occurs at 00:13:00 through 00:16:00.

The scene of Hera deeming a human death unimportant occurs at 00:05:00.

The scenes of Zeus and Perseus discussing destiny occur at 00:25:00 and 00:34:00.

The scene of Thetis asking Zeus to forgive her son Calibos occurs at 00:14:00.

The scene of Perseus battling Medusa occurs at 01:28:00.

Instructor Viewing Information

Clash of the Titans (1981) is the last feature film for which Ray Harryhausen created the special effects. Harryhausen used stop motion animation for Medusa, the full shots of Calibos, and many of the creatures in the film. Students may find the special effects unimpressive by today's standards, so some context may be needed. Students may also find the film slow and plodding in parts, but should enjoy the exciting fight sequences. While *Clash of the Titans* (1981) combines characters from Greek mythology with characters made up for the film, it provides a good starting point for examining the relationship between the gods and mortals. The film also provides a good way to introduce the concept of myth and the insights myths provide.

Synopsis

The film begins with Zeus (Olivier) protecting the infant Perseus and his mother. At the same time, Zeus punishes Calibos (McCarthy) for squandering his life by transforming him into a shunned and deformed creature doomed to live in the swamp. Zeus uses wooden figures that represent humans and moves them as he wills. Thetis (Smith) is angry that Zeus will not protect her son Calibos the way Zeus protected his own child Perseus. Thetis, also angry that her son will no longer be able to marry Andromeda (Bowker), decrees that no man shall have her. Perseus (Hamlin) grows to a strong young man and meets wise Ammon (Meredith). Ammon tells him that no man may marry Andromeda until they answer her riddle. Zeus provides Perseus with a sword, shield, and helmet that render him invisible. Perseus answers the riddle and injures Calibos in fight. As Perseus and Andromeda prepare to wed, Andromeda's mother Cassiopeia (Phillips) angers Thetis by comparing her daughter's beauty to that of Thetis. Thetis decrees that Andromeda must be sacrificed as a virgin to the Kraken. Peruses goes on a quest to defeat the Kraken. He kills Calibos, cuts off Medusa's head, and uses it to destroy the Kraken. Perseus and

Andromeda wed. The film ends with Zeus decreeing that Peruses should be rewarded with a happy life with Andromeda. Zeus commands that Perseus, Andromeda, and Cassiopeia will be set upon the stars and constellations to perpetuate the story of Perseus' courage.

Discussion Questions

1. **Explain how the film shows Zeus to be a womanizer.**

   The film briefly touches on Zeus' many wives and lovers. Zeus' womanizing is established in the start of the film by a conversation between Hera and Thetis. They laughingly discuss Zeus' predilection for seducing both moral and immortal women while in disguise. Hera and Thetis scoff at the idea that Zeus has any feelings for Perseus' mother by saying that Zeus has known so many women that he cannot possibly remember them all. However in the remainder of the film, Zeus has no romantic interactions with either mortal or immortal women. In fact, his interactions with the immortal women are confined to giving these women orders.

2. **Describe how the film portrays the relationship between gods and humans.**

   In the film, the gods manipulate the lives of humans, but humans ultimately choose their own destiny. At the beginning of the film, we see that Zeus has miniature clay models of humans on shelves in a cabinet. Both Zeus and Thetis pick up models of the humans to affect the direction of their lives. Although the film portrays the Greek gods, this scene with the clay models comes closer to reflecting the Roman view of the gods as implacable forces that limit or even destroy the freedom of human beings. Zeus urges Perseus to find his own destiny, and Perseus talks about finding his destiny. However, Thetis moves Perseus to put him in danger, and Zeus moves Perseus to protect him. Nevertheless, Perseus survives by using his wit and skills and by choosing his own actions. Hera disagrees with the decree to punish those who intend to kill Perseus and his mother. She dismisses the importance of the impending human death, saying that what is important is to protect those humans who built many temples to the gods. But Zeus contradicts this idea at the end of the film.

3. **Describe how the film portrays the relationship between the gods and their children.**

   In the film, the gods are very protective of their human child. The film shows no rivalries or jealousies between father and son, or mother and son. Zeus protects his human son

Perseus again and again. If fact, he is willing to destroy humans who worship him loyally because they tried to harm Perseus. Thetis' motivation for trying to harm Perseus is anger at Zeus for deforming her human son Calibos. When Thetis begs Zeus to forgive her son Calibos and Zeus refuses, Thetis states that had it been Zeus' son Perseus, Zeus would have granted forgiveness. At the end of the film, Zeus shows his love for Perseus and Perseus' family by granting them a long and happy life and placing their likenesses in the stars.

5. *Clash of the Titans* (2010)

Film Data

Year: 2010

Director: Louis Leterrier

Length: 106 minutes

Rated: PG-13

Characters/Actors

Perseus:	Sam Worthington
Zeus:	Liam Neeson
Hades:	Ralph Fiennes
Calibos/Acrisius:	Jason Flemyng
Io:	Gemma Arterton
Andromeda:	Alexa Davalos
Cassiopeia:	Polly Walker
Draco:	Mads Mikkelsen

Connection to Chapters

Chapter 3. Greece: Hesiod

Chapter 32. Greece: Heracles and Dionysus

Recommended Scenes

The scene of Perseus' adopted father railing against the gods occurs at 00:06:00.

The scene of Zeus expressing his anger at humans occurs at 00:10:00.

The scene of the King and Queen of Argos proclaiming a new era of man occurs at 00:16:00 through 00:19:00.

The scene of Io telling Perseus the story of his birth occurs at 00:24:00 through 00:27:00.

The scene of Perseus and his men talking about the gods occurs at 00:53:00 through 00:55:00.

The scene of Zeus and Hades arguing about man occurs at 01:26:00.

The scene of Zeus discussing Hades and man's fate with Perseus occurs at 01:34:00.

Instructor Viewing Information

Clash of the Titans (2010) is a remake of the 1981 film. The plot is somewhat different than the first film, and students may find the plot less convoluted and easier to follow. While the special effects are less compelling, students may enjoy this more recent version. The film emphasizes the role of free will and the adversarial nature of the relationship between the gods and man. *Clash of the Titans* (2010) should provide a good way to discuss the complexities of the relationship between the gods and man, the role of fate, and the ancient Greeks' view of free will.

Synopsis

King Acrisius (Flemyng) is angry at the gods for their poor treatment of humans. But Zeus (Neeson) loves man too much to punish them with destruction. Instead, Zeus makes an example of Acrisius by disguising himself as king and impregnating the queen. When the real king discovers this, he orders his wife and the infant Perseus executed. They are cast into the sea and Perseus' mother perishes, but Perseus survives. Perseus is adopted by the loving fisherman who finds him. Perseus' adopted father rails against the gods for the poor conditions present in human life. Zeus is again angry at humans for their disloyalty. Hades (Fiennes), brother of Zeus, encourages Zeus to let him lose on humanity so that humans will again worship the gods. Meanwhile, Perseus (Worthington) grows to be a strong man who is angry at the gods for killing his adopted parents. He joins an army in Argos, where Queen Cassiopeia (Walker) angers the gods. Hades swoops into Argos and tells them he will unleash the Kraken to destroy them all, unless Andromeda (Davalos) is sacrificed. However, Hades is plotting with Acrisius, who has become the monster Calibos, against Zeus. Perseus meets Io (Arterton), who tells him the story of his heritage. Perseus begins a journey to defeat the Kraken. Perseus repeatedly stated that he wishes to be a man, not a god, and initially refuses help from Zeus. Perseus eventually accepts a sword and Pegasus from Zeus, and leads men into battle to destroy the Kraken. He battles Calicos and finally kills him, visits the witches, and takes his men to the underworld to obtain the head of Medusa. Zeus visits Perseus again and offers him a home as a god in Olympus. Perseus still prefers being a man. Perseus uses the head of Medusa to defeat the Kraken and then sends Hades back to the underworld. The film ends with Zeus praising Perseus.

Discussion Questions

1. **Explain how the film portrays the attitude of humans toward the gods.**

   Throughout the film, the gods are seen as vengeful and petty, while the humans are imbued with nobility. *Clash of the Titans* (2010) begins with Acrisius blaming the gods for the poor quality of human lives. Perseus' adopted father also blames the gods for his misery and tells Perseus that one day, someone must make a stand against the gods. Cassiopeia proclaims a new era for man, and says that gods need humans to worship them more than humans need gods. Perseus tells Zeus that he would prefer to be man, and declines Zeus' offer to live as a god on Olympus. When Perseus in infected with poison, he refuses to pray to Zeus. Perseus initially refuses to accept Zeus' gift of weapons, not wanting to owe the gods a debt and preferring to do battle as a man. During the battle, Perseus' men extol the values of humanity and talk about spitting in the eye of the gods. The men in battle pledge their loyalty to Perseus, saying that it was a man who saved their lives, not the gods. When Perseus finally defeats Calibos/Acrisius, the monster regains his human form and tells Perseus not "to become one of them." At the end of the film, when Perseus is aware that he is half-god and half-human, he still chooses to live a man.

2. **Explain how the film portrays the attitude of the gods toward humans.**

   Through most of the film, the relationship between gods and humans is adversarial. Zeus appears to not care about humans, but his position softens toward the end of the film. The film begins with Zeus expressing his anger at humans. Even though Hades tells Zeus that Zeus loves humans too much, Zeus allows himself to be convinced to unleash the Kraken on humanity. When humanity may be destroyed by Hades, Zeus assists Perseus by providing him with weapons and help from Io. However, it is unclear if Zeus is motivated to help mankind because he loves humans or if he just wants his son Perseus to survive. Later on, Zeus explains that the gods needed to find a way to make humans worship them again. Near the end of the *Clash of the Titans* (2010), Zeus states that the gods need the love of humans. Zeus also tells Perseus that people may want to worship him, and that he hopes Perseus will treat humans better than the gods treated humans.

3. **Describe how the film portrays the relationship between the god Zeus and his human son Perseus.**

In the beginning of the film, Zeus dismisses the importance of his son Perseus. He tells the other gods that Perseus is no different than other human beings, as he has never heard Perseus pray to him. However, Zeus provides Perseus with weapons to use in battle, as well as Pegasus and a gold coin. Zeus also invites Perseus to take his rightful place as a god, but respects his decision to remain a man. Near the end of the film, Zeus makes it clear that he loves Perseus when he tells Perseus that he wanted mankind to worship the gods again, but not at the expense of his son. Zeus also shows his love for Perseus by bringing Io back to life, so that Perseus will not be alone.

4. **Describe how the film shows the role of fate and free will.**

The characters in this film talk about fate, but although the gods influence humans, the humans appear to have free will. In a brief scene in the film Zeus handles a clay figure of Perseus, but the gods here seem to have less control over human actions that in the previous version of this film. Zeus does help Perseus in battle, but Perseus makes his own choices, even choosing to remain a mortal. Io tells Perseus that he was born to end tyranny, and that appears to be his path. Io also tells Perseus that the fate of Argos is in his hands. When Hades and Zeus argue about man near the end of the film, Zeus tells Hades that he hopes Perseus will save man. The gods appear to be watching and helping a little, but man determines his own fate. At the end of the film, Zeus tells Perseus that it will be up to man to determine if Hades will return.

6. The Fisher King

Film Data

Year: 1991

Director: Terry Gilliam

Length: 137 minutes

Rated: R

Characters/Actors

Jeff Bridges: Jack

Mercedes Ruehl: Anne

Robin Williams: Parry

Amanda Plummer: Lydia

Michael Jeter: Homeless Cabaret Singer

Connection to Chapters

Part III. Heroes and Tricksters: Introductory Overview

Chapter 15. Theory: Joseph Campbell, *The Hero with a Thousand Faces* (Dave Whomsley)

Chapter 42. *Harry Potter:* A Rankian Analysis of the Hero of Hogwarts

Recommended Scenes

The scene of Parry rescuing Jack occurs at 00:17:42 through 00:21:01.

The scene of Parry telling Jack that Jack is the chosen one occurs at 00:23:55 through 00:28:16.

The scene of Jack learning Parry's true identity occurs at 00:35:17 through 00:36:20.

The scene of Parry telling Jack the story of the Fisher King occurs at 01:00:28 through 01:02:55.

The scene of Jack and Anne's double date with Lydia and Parry and Parry's attack and comatose state occurs at 01:27:22 through 01:42:00.

The scene of Jack retrieving the "Holy Grail" and Parry recovering occurs at 01:59:55 through 02:10:11.

Instructor Viewing Information

The Fisher King features outstanding performances by lead actors Jeff Bridges and Robin Williams, as well as Mercedes Ruehl, who won an Academy Award for her performance as Anne. Students should be familiar with Bridges and Williams and should enjoy the comedy in the film, as well as the more serious elements of the plot. The film deals with contemporary issues such as the power of the media and gun violence. These issues should resonate with students, and should work nicely with a discussion of older myths. *The Fisher King* will provide a good way to discuss Campbell's ideas about heroes, the use of myth in modern films, and the themes of heroes and rebirth.

Synopsis

Jack (Bridges), a successful radio shock-jock, is self-involved and callous. He is seems headed for television success when some ill-advised words to a caller to the show change his life. The caller shoots and kills patrons in an upscale bar, and then shoots himself. The film then jumps to Jack's life three years later. Jack lives above a video store owned by his girlfriend Anne (Ruehl). He drinks heavily and is depressed. While wandering drunk, a gang of boys mistakes Jack for a homeless drunk and tries to set him on fire. Jack is saved by a group of homeless men dressed as knights, led by Parry (Williams). Parry believes he is a knight on a quest to find the Holy Grail, and that Jack has been sent to help him. When Jack learns that Parry became insane after Parry's wife was shot and killed in the upscale bar shooting, Jack feels obligated to help Parry. Jack and Anne help Parry woo Lydia (Plummer), the girl Parry loves from afar. Jack feels so good about helping Parry that he tries to return to his career and leaves his girlfriend. Just when things are looking better for Parry, Parry is beaten up and slips into a catatonic state. Doctors believe he is re-experiencing his original trauma. Jack visits Parry, but it appears Jack has returned to his old life and former self, when his conscience is reawakened. Jack steals the cup Parry believes is the Holy Grail from an Upper East Side apartment and gives it to Parry. Parry comes out of the catatonic state and resumes his romance with Lydia. Jack admits he loves Anne and they reconcile. Both men are better for the experience of knowing each other, and the film ends with Jack and Parry in Central Park.

1. **Explain how both Jack and Parry take some of the steps in the hero's journey as outlined by Campbell.**

Parry believes he saw a vision of little people floating before his eyes. He believes they sent him a sign, which directed him to page in an architecture book. There he sees a picture of a cup he believes to be the Holy Grail on a bookshelf in a room in an Upper East Side apartment. Parry tells Jack that Jack has been sent to help him on the quest. Jack at first refuses to help Parry, explaining that he is not the one. When Jack learns that Parry's wife was a victim of the shooting, Jack changes his mind. For Jack, the adventure is to help Parry and ease his own conscience. At first, Jack refuses this call to adventure. He tries to give Parry money, which Parry does not want. Jack comes to understand that the real quest is being involved in Parry's life and helping Parry. Jack and Anne accomplish this together by arranging a double date with Parry and Lydia. Jack wants to achieve forgiveness and redemption. Parry wants to triumph over his delusion of the red knight, who represents Parry's traumatic memories of his wife's murder. Through most of the film, we see their road of trials. Near the end of the film, Jack must choose between his old life and being a better person. He chooses to help Parry by scaling the Upper East Side tower and stealing the cup Parry believes to be the Holy Grail. In doing so, Jack also saves the life of the owner of the apartment. Parry must battle his way out of his comatose state and the weight of his traumatic memories. When Jack gives Parry the cup, Parry awakens from his state and resumes his life. For both men the cup symbolizes the illumination each gained at the end of their adventure. Parry accepts the painful memories he has and continues his romance with Lydia. Jack faces the truth about his life and redefines his values. He becomes a more caring person, admits he loves Anne, and accepts his responsibility toward Parry. By the end of the film, both men are not only wiser, but happier.

2. **Describe how the film shows Jack experiencing a rebirth.**

At the start of the film, we see that Jack cares only for himself. He lives in a high-rise apartment with his cold girlfriend. He refuses to give money to a homeless person. He only cares about his career and his upcoming audition. When he gives advice to a disturbed caller, he is callous and unfeeling. He treats the call as a comedy routine for his show, never taking the caller seriously. After the caller kills several people, Jack becomes a depressed drunk. It is unclear if he feels guilty about the tragedy or if he feels depressed because it damaged his career. Three years after the shooting, Jack sponges off his girlfriend and wanders the streets. As he helps Parry, he meets other homeless people, including a cabaret singer in drag (Jeter). When Jack asks the singer to help him, he muses that he cannot believe he is on a first-name basis with such people. But this is the beginning of Jack's rebirth. When Jack helps Parry date Lydia, Anne is proud of him. When Jack has the opportunity to revitalize his career and return to his old life, he briefly gives in to that temptation. When the homeless singer is being arrested by the police and calls Jack by name, Jack pretends not to know him. But overcome with guilt, Jack leaves his meeting and visits Parry in the hospital. He risks his life to retrieve a cup for Parry. By the end of the film, Jack is a different person. He has been reborn into a man who cares about others.

3. Describe how the film shows the importance of hero myths to the characters.

Before the shooting, Parry was a happily married college professor. The film shows his life after his tragedy. Parry has blocked out most memories of his old life. However, in the middle of the film, Parry shares a memory with Jack. Parry tells Jack that he remembers being at a lecture (probably an academic conference) and hearing the story of the Fisher King. He tells Jack his version of the tale. As Parry talks about the king, the Holy Grail that could heal the hearts of men, and the empathy of the fool, we see how important the myth is to Parry. It is one of the few connections to his old life that he holds close. His mental delusions allow Parry to imagine that he is a brave knight searching for the Holy Grail and that Jack has been chosen to help him. The power of the story changes both of their lives. Jack and Parry both need the empathy of the fool and the bravery of a hero. Each provides empathy and bravery for the other. When Jack breaks into the apartment to steal the cup, he is reminded of the tale of the Fisher King. He sees the billionaire owner of the place unconscious with a glass beside him. As Jack leaves with the cup, he intentionally sets off the alarm, so the man's life can be saved. Jack found the "Holy Grail," saves a stranger's life, and saves Parry's life. By doing so, he also saves his own life, by becoming a better person.

7. Harry Potter and the Sorcerer's Stone

Film Data

Year: 2001

Director: Chris Columbus

Length: 152 minutes

Rated: PG

Characters/Actors

Richard Harris: Professor Albus Dumbledore

Maggie Smith: Professor Minerva McGonagall

Robbie Coltrane: Rubeus Hagrid

Daniel Radcliffe: Harry Potter

Rupert Grint: Ron Weasley

Emma Watson: Hermione Granger

Richard Bremmer: He Who Must Not Be Named

Fiona Shaw: Aunt Petunia Dursley

Harry Melling: Dudley Dursley

Geraldine Somerville: Lily Potter

Connection to Chapters

Chapter 42. *Harry Potter:* A Rankian Analysis of the Hero of Hogwarts

Recommended Scenes

The scene in the wand shop occurs at 00:25:21 through 00:28:38.

The scene of Hermione telling Harry his parents were seekers occurs at 01:27:00.The scene of the Quidditch match occurs at 01:20:14 through 01:23:09.

The scene of Harry seeing his parents in the mirror occurs at 01:32:54 through 01:36:12.

The scene of the battle with He Who Must Not Be Named (Voldemort) occurs at 02:08:43 through 02:13:57.

The scene of Dumbledore explaining what happened to Harry occurs at 02:15:00 through 02:16:51.

The scene of Hagrid saying goodbye to Harry occurs at 02:21:50 through the end of the film.

Instructor Viewing Information

Most students will be quite familiar with the story and characters in *Harry Potter and the Sorcerer's Stone*. Students should find the film very enjoyable. The film provides an excellent companion to the material discussed by Grimes. *Harry Potter and the Sorcerer's Stone* contains rich examples of positive and negative mother and father figures. The film should provide a very enjoyable way to discuss Grimes' theories about using Rank's analysis for Harry Potter.

Synopsis

Harry Potter (Radcliffe) lives with his mean aunt, uncle, and cousin. On his eleventh birthday, Rubeus Hagrid (Coltrane) tells him that he is really a wizard and his parents were killed by the evil He Who Must Not Be Named (Bremmer). Hagrid takes Harry to Hogwarts to learn magic. Along the way, Harry befriends fellow students Ron Weasley (Grint) and Hermione Granger (Watson). The three friends study potions, play Quidditch, and explore their magical surroundings. They learn that someone is trying to steal the sorcerer's stone, which can grant immortality. The three friends have several adventures, culminating in an encounter with a three-headed dog followed by a dangerous game of chess. After Ron is injured, Harry alone must face He Who Must Not Be Named. Harry retrieves the stone, and the evil one is defeated for the time being. The film ends with Harry and his friends successfully completing their first year at Hogwarts. The students go home for the summer, but Harry knows that Hogwarts is his real home.

Discussion Questions

1. **Describe how the film illustrates Grimes' ideas about positive father figures.**

    Harry's positive father figures are both magical and ordinary. Harry learns that his biological father was a powerful wizard. Although he cannot remember his father, he loves him and wishes to learn more about him. When Harry is asked to be a seeker in Quidditch, he is nervous about failing. Hermione informs Harry that his parents were seekers and that being good at it is in his blood. Later, Harry sees an image of his dead parents in the Mirror of Erised, which reveals one's deepest desires. Harry's deepest desire is to be with his father and mother. Professor Albus Dumbledore (Harris) acts as a magical father figure for Harry. Dumbledore provides Harry with protection and advice. Dumbledore uses magic in arranging for Hagrid to bring Harry to live with his aunt and uncle, saying it is best for him to grow up away from magic, until he is ready to be a wizard. When Harry and Ron worry that Voldemort might try to kill Harry, Hermione explains that Dumbledore is the one wizard whom Voldemort fears. She reasons that as long as Dumbledore is around, Harry is safe. When Harry sees his parents in the mirror, Dumbledore explains the dangers of dwelling on dreams and forgetting to live. Near the end of the film, Dumbledore is in the infirmary when Harry wakes up. He explains to Harry what happened with the stone and tells Harry why he survived. Hagrid is an ordinary father figure who operates in a magical world. He is big, funny, and kind, although not brilliant like Dumbledore. Hagrid is the one entrusted by Dumbledore to bring baby Harry to Dumbledore before Harry is given to his uncle and aunt. Hagrid cries when he leaves Harry. Hagrid also retrieves Harry from his aunt and uncle. Hagrid tells Harry about his parents. Hagrid performs the more mundane, but important, jobs of a father. He takes Harry shopping for his wand and other magical school supplies. At the end of the film, Hagrid walks Harry to the train. He shows he understands Harry's emotional needs when he gives Harry a moving picture album of Harry's parents. He also gives Harry some advice about standing up to Harry's bully of a cousin.

2. **Describe how the film illustrates Grimes' ideas about negative father figures.**

    Harry's negative father figures are also both ordinary and magical. Harry's Uncle Dudley Dursley (Melling) treats Harry with contempt and attempts to squash his magical abilities. He burns his letters from Hogwarts and conceals the truth about Harry's magical parents. When Hagrid arrives, the Dursleys try to stop Harry from going to Hogwarts, calling magic "rubbish." Voldemort is Harry Potter's magical negative father figure. Several scenes in the film emphasize the numerous ties between Harry and Voldemort. When Harry's wand chooses him, he learns from the shopkeeper that Harry's wand has a twin wand owned by Voldemort. It was Voldemort's wand that gave Harry his scar. The shopkeeper tells Harry that although Voldemort was evil, he did great things, and that he expects Harry to do great things. Hagrid tells Harry that he is "the boy that lived." While Harry's parents were killed by Voldemort, infant Harry survived the attack. As the only person who survived an encounter with Voldemort, Harry is famous and Voldemort wants to kill him. When Harry encounters Voldemort at the end of the film, Voldemort tries to get Harry to join him on the dark side. When Harry refuses, Voldemort tries to kill him, but Harry survives. As representatives of good and evil, Harry and Voldemort repel and attract each other.

3. **Explain how the film shows Grimes' updating of Rank's ideas regarding mother figures.**

Lily (Somerville), Harry's biological mother, is very important to him. Like his father, Lily was also magical. When Harry sees his parents in the Mirror of Erised, he sees his mother touching his shoulder. His deepest wish is for his mother's love. Near the end of the film, Harry learns from Dumbledore that his mother sacrificed herself to save him. Dumbledore explains that love like that leaves a mark. This is why Harry's touch burned Voldemort. Lily continues to protect Harry, even though she is dead. Professor Minerva McGonagall (Smith) also acts as a mother figure here. She disguises herself as a cat so she can join Dumbledore when they put baby Harry on the Dursleys' doorstep. She worries about Harry like a mother would, as she tells Dumbledore that she has been watching the house all day and that the Dursleys are "the worst sort of Muggles." She also is stern but fair with Harry and punishes him when he breaks the rules.

8. Hercules

Film Data

Year: 1959

Director: Pietro Francisci

Length: 107 minutes

Rated: PG

Characters/Actors

Hercules: Steve Reeves

Iole: Sylva Koscina

Jason: Fabrizio Mioni

Pelias: Ivo Garrani

Antea, Queen of the Amazons: Gianna Maria Canale

Connection to Chapters

Chapter 32. Greece: Heracles and Dionysus

Recommended Scenes

The scene of Hercules training the young men of Iolcus occurs at 00:19:40.

The scene of Hercules discussing his destiny with the oracle occurs at 00:35:32.

The scene of Iole and Hercules discussing their new destinies occurs at 00:49:11.

The scene of Jason discussing his father's wishes and his conscience with Hercules occurs at 01:29:55.

Instructor Viewing Information

Hercules is the dubbed version of the 1958 Italian film *Le fatiche di Ercole*. Even American bodybuilder Steve Reeves is dubbed. Students may find unintended humor in the overly dramatic dialogue and acting, so some introduction to the film may be needed. Although the plot is somewhat convoluted, students should enjoy the exciting action sequences. While *Hercules* combines characters and events from several stories, the film does refer to three of the labors of Hercules. The film's view of Hercules as a monogamous and moral individual who wishes to live a traditional mortal life provides a good starting point for examining the many facets of the character of Hercules.

Synopsis

Hercules (Reeves) arrives in Iolcus after saving the life of Iole (Koscina), the scantily clad daughter of King Pelias (Garrani). He is viewed with suspicion by the king, but is hailed as hero by the young men in the kingdom, and they attempt to emulate his strength and prowess. Hercules and Iole fall in love, but their romance is soon interrupted. Hercules kills a deadly lion, defeats the Cretan bull, and helps Jason (Mioni) reclaim his throne from evil King Pelias. Along the way, Hercules proclaims his desire to live as a mortal and have a family. After Jason and his men succumb to the charms of Antea, Queen of the Amazons (Canale), and her Amazonian women, Hercules rescues them and returns with Jason to Iolcus. Jason takes his rightful places as king, and Hercules and Iole embrace.

Discussion Questions

1. **Explain how the film shows Hercules to be more than just a powerful and savage warrior.**

   The film begins with Hercules lifting a tree to prevent Iole's runaway horses from killing her. He then roasts a large piece of meat over a fire and eats it without cutting it. That is the only hint in this film of Hercules' savage or boorish nature. When challenged, Hercules easily bests the most powerful men in Iolcus in contests requiring physical prowess. Hercules only uses violence when needed to save his life or the lives of others. After a man-eating lion kills several people, Hercules races off to chase the lion. After killing the lion, Hercules expresses regret that he is unable to save Iole's brother from the lion. Hercules defeats the Cretan bull, but only after being ordered to by an oracle.

2. **Describe how Hercules is a role model for young men.**

The young men of Iolcus train for marathons until they need medical assistance. The elders remark that since Hercules arrived, the young men worship strength and neglect their studies. Hercules encourages the young men to emulate him, and they bask in his praise. While some of the elders worry that Hercules could lead the younger men in battle against them, most are glad to have Hercules on their side. A young man training with Hercules tells him that all the young men know Hercules wants them to use their strength to serve their intelligence. Hercules agrees that strength alone is not enough. He teaches strategy along with physical skill.

3. **Describe how the film portrays Hercules' sexuality.**

Despite some initial suggestive flirting with Iole, Hercules is rather chaste here. He engages in passionate kisses with Iole and tries to reason with her when she is angry with him for his actions against her family. He treats her with politeness and respect. He declares his love for Iole and remains faithful to her throughout the film. Unlike the other men in his company, he even resists the temptation of the Amazon women. Hercules even rails at the gods, proclaiming his desire to have a family and watch his children grow. He would rather not be a superior being and instead professes a desire to live a more traditional mortal life.

4. **What role do destiny and free will play in the lives of the characters?**

Hercules is told to continue obeying the gods and not to rebel against his fate. Hercules instead uses his free will and asks to be made mortal. When his wish is granted, he finds he still must kill the Cretan bull as the gods ordered. But the oracle tells him he can follow his destiny wherever he likes and risk punishment from the gods. Hercules expresses gratitude that he may choose his own destiny. Jason is told that it is his destiny to take over his throne without violence, and then finds a message from his dead father asking the same. Jason resists the urge to take vengeance on his father's killer. He tells Hercules he must obey both his father's wishes and his own conscience. But Jason and Hercules are attacked, and they must fight for Jason to reclaim his throne. Hercules tells Iole that it is their shared destiny to find the truth about her uncle's death, but Iole replies that she and Hercules no longer have the same destiny. At the end of the film, Iole receives her father's blessing to go with Hercules. Hercules and Iole choose to have a new life and leave together.

9. *Hercules* (animated)

Film Data

Year: 1997

Director: Ron Clements and John Musker

Length: 93 minutes

Rated: G

Characters/Actors

Tate Donovan:	Hercules (voice)
Josh Keaton:	Young Hercules (singing voice)
Danny DeVito:	Philoctetes (voice)
James Woods:	Hades, Lord of the Underworld (voice)
Rip Torn:	Zeus (voice)
Samantha Eggar:	Hera, Hercules' Mother (voice)
Susan Egan:	Meg (voice)

Connection to Chapters

Chapter 15. Theory: Joseph Campbell, *The Hero with a Thousand Faces* (Dave Whomsley)

Chapter 32. Greece: Heracles and Dionysus

Recommended Scenes

The scene of the witches making a prediction for Hades occurs at 00:09:20.

The scene of Zeus and Hercules being reunited occurs at 00:21:35.

The scene of the gospel song about Hercules' adventures as a hero occurs at 00:48:53.

The scene of the reference to Hercules' labors occurs at 00:54:49 through 00:55:39.

The scene of Hercules and Hades making the deal for Meg's life occurs at 1:08:35.

The scene of Hercules offering to trade his life for Meg's life and rescuing Meg from the underworld occurs at 1:21:00.

The scene of Hercules returning to Zeus and Hera with Meg and resolving his adventure occurs at 1:23:57.

Instructor Viewing Information

Hercules is an animated Disney musical with gospel-style music by frequent Disney composer Alan Menken and lyrics by David Zippel. The film tells a story that features some of the characters in the Heracles myth. Although many details have been changed to make the story appropriate for children, the film contains sly references and humor that adults will appreciate. Students should enjoy the popular culture references as well as the irreverent and comical tone. While the film does not deal directly with the labors of Heracles, *Hercules* should be an enjoyable way to introduce the material about Heracles. The film is also a good way to illustrate the many ways Joseph Campbell's ideas about heroes are found in old myths and contemporary retellings.

Synopsis

Hercules (Donovan) is the beloved son of Zeus (Torn) and Hera (Eggar). The three witches tell the evil Hades (Woods) to release the titans in eighteen years. They predict that Zeus will fall and Hades will be victorious, but if Hercules fights, Hades will fall. Hades sends a potion to harm Hercules. Hercules is made mortal and is adopted by a childless couple. However, because Hercules did not drink the last drop of the potion, he retains his strength. Hercules grows up and meets his true parents. Zeus tells Hercules that he cannot return to Olympus until he proves that he is a true hero. Philoctetes (DeVito) trains Hercules to be a hero. Hercules performs many brave deeds, including rescuing the lovely Meg (Eggar). But Meg is working for Hades to discover Hercules' weakness. Meg and Hercules fall in love and she eventually helps Hercules. Meg gets hurt, her agreement with Hades is invalidated, and Hercules becomes a god. Hades traps Meg in the underworld, and Hercules offers to trade his life for Meg's. Hercules survives the underworld because he is a god, and rescues Meg. Hercules and Zeus return to Olympus. Zeus proclaims that Hercules is a true hero because he was willing to sacrifice his life for Meg's. Hercules chooses to stay with Meg and remain mortal. They kiss and live happily on earth.

Discussion Questions

1. **Explain how the film portrays Hercules' many-sided personality.**

The film shows Hercules to be a bit of a cultural hero. However, the film presents Hercules as more of an icon than a role model. The film shows this in the gospel song "Zero to Hero." The song chronicles Hercules' rise to fame. Hercules is shown making money for personal appearances, enjoying the adoration of women, and seeing his likeness on vases. We even see a credit card with his name. At a Hercules merchandise store, statues of Hercules are a popular item. Hercules is likened to a celebrity, with merchandise bearing his name and likeness. He has no interaction with those young men who look up to him. We never see him training young men or passing on his skill. Although Hercules brags to Zeus about his adventures, the actual twelve labors of Hercules are never shown, and are only obliquely referred to by Philoctetes. Hercules falls in love with Meg, but their relationship is rather chaste. Hercules' womanizing and sexuality is nonexistent in this child-friendly film. The same can be said of violent behavior. Hercules finds the skill to defeat those who attack him and others, but he never seems to enjoy savage acts. Hercules' reputation as a drunken buffoon is changed here, and he is portrayed as a somewhat good-natured oaf. His immense strength leads him to accidentally break things. The other children make fun of him for being different, and a sensitive Hercules says that he longs to be like everyone else.

2. **Describe how the film portrays the power and personality of the gods and the relationship between the gods and humans.**

In this version of the myth, Hercules' father is still Zeus, but his mother is Zeus' wife Hera. Here, Zeus is not a womanizer and Hera is not jealous. Zeus and Hera are shown to be loving, gentle, and proud parents. Zeus is an older man with a white flowing beard, and is well liked. Zeus does not seem to meddle in the affairs of humans. When Hercules is made mortal, Zeus can do nothing to reverse this. We are told that the mortal Hercules can never return home, and heartbroken Zeus and Hera may only watch from afar. The gods also seem as powerless against fate as mortals. When Hades is told that he will only defeat Zeus if Hercules does not fight, he accepts this and sets out to destroy Hercules. Hades is not powerful enough to kill the mortal Hercules on his own, and must enlist the help of a mortal woman, Meg. When Zeus and Hercules are reunited, Zeus tells Hercules that his status as a god will be restored if he becomes a true hero and tells him to seek out Philoctetes. Zeus also gives Hercules Pegasus. The gods provide advice and gifts, but it is up to Hercules to forge his own path. Later, Zeus tells Hercules that being famous is not the same as being a hero. Zeus is shown to have a sense of morality, which he wants to pass on to his son. At the end of the film, when Hercules tells Zeus that he wishes to stay on earth with Meg, Hera and Zeus smile proudly. Like human parents, the gods want their child to be happy.

3. **Describe how the film shows Hercules following the steps of Campbell's hero's journey.**

Hercules is called to adventure by destiny. He finds out his true parents are gods and leaves his home in search of them. When he encounters Zeus, Zeus tells him he must be a hero to return to Olympus. Hercules has two protective figures here. He is provided with advice from Zeus as well as Pegasus, a type of supernatural weapon. Zeus' advice causes Hercules to seek out Philoctetes, a wiser and older trainer of heroes. Philoctetes teaches Hercules how to fight effectively and offers encouragement. Hercules has many adventures and trials here, and is successful in all of them. When Hades traps Meg in the underworld, Hercules offers to trade his life for hers. Near the end of the film, Hercules goes to the underworld to rescue Meg. Hercules is in the "belly of the whale" by being swallowed up into another world. Hercules succeeds in rescuing Meg and emerges unharmed from the underworld. Hercules is greeted with applause and love by Hera and Zeus on Mount Olympus. They tell him that by risking his life to save Meg's, he is a true hero, since a hero is not measured by the size of his strength, but by the strength of his heart. Hercules is now raised to the stature of god. At the end of the film, Hercules learns from his adventure and achieves illumination and a new understanding of his life. He realizes that he wishes to stay on earth with Meg. Hercules tells Zeus that he finally knows where he belongs.

10. I Am Legend

Film Data

Year: 2007

Director: Francis Lawrence

Length: 101 minutes

Rated: PG-13

Characters/Actors

Will Smith: Robert Neville

Alice Braga: Anna

Charlie Tahan: Ethan

Connection to Chapters

Chapter 13. The Bible: Genesis (Flood)

Chapter 15. Theory: Joseph Campbell, *The Hero with a Thousand Faces* (Dave Whomsley)

Chapter 41. *Stagecoach* and *Firefly:* The Journey into the Unknown in Westerns and Science Fiction

Recommended Scenes

The scene of Neville getting his family out of New York occurs at 00:13:04 through 00:15:11.

The scene of Neville and Sam being attacked by zombies and Neville experimenting on a zombie occurs at 00:31:20 through 00:37:40.

The scene of Neville first talking to Anna about the virus occurs at 01:05:54 through 01:13:47.

The scene of Neville discussing Bob Marley with Anna and Anna discussing God's plan occurs at 01:16:16 through 01:20:13.

The scene of the final battle with the zombies and the resolution of the story occurs at 01:26:36 through the end of the film.

Instructor Viewing Information

I Am Legend is based on the 1954 novel written by Richard Matheson. The film features a strong performance by Will Smith; most of the film consists of Smith's character talking to his dog and himself. The film moves at quick pace, and students should enjoy the apocalyptic story, sympathetic main character, and zombie fight scenes. The film should be an effective and enjoyable way to begin discussing destruction myths. *I Am Legend* also provides a good example of some of the steps of a hero's journey as described Joseph Campbell. This film should also be a good way to explore the way this contemporary futuristic film reflects the concerns of its audience.

Synopsis

Robert Neville (Smith) seems to be the only person left in New York City. Flashback scenes reveal that three years after a cure for cancer was found, a byproduct of the cure caused a deadly virus. Most of those infected die, and the others become vicious killers who look and act like zombies. Only a small percentage of the population is immune. Neville is immune. He was an army colonel and scientist who worked on the cure. He tried to help his wife and children escape a quarantined Manhattan, but his family was killed. Now he spends his days working on a cure for the virus, looking for other human survivors, and walking with his dog Sam. The zombie creatures cannot stand light, but roam the streets when the sun goes down. Neville spends his nights in his locked house. He meets Anna (Braga), a young woman traveling with a young boy Ethan (Tahan), after they save Neville's life. Anna tells him about a colony of survivors in Vermont. At first, Neville does not believe her. After the creatures break into the house, Neville, Anna, and Ethan hide in Neville's lab. While there, Anna notices that a zombie test subject shows signs of returning to her human form. Neville gives Anna the subject's blood containing the cure for the virus and tells her to take it to Vermont. Neville stays in the lab and uses a grenade to kill the zombies and kills himself. The film ends with Anna reaching the colony with the cure and seeing other humans. She explains that Neville gave his life to save humanity.

Discussion Questions

1. **Explain how the film reflects the concerns of its audience.**

   Neville refers to the city as "ground zero" several times during the film. Of course, this term was used often after the events of September 11 in New York. The idea of a destroyed New York City would have special meaning in the years following the Twin Towers tragedy. The sight of a deserted Times Square is especially potent. Neville refers to the virus as something that is the fault of man. Here, the film hints at a fear many have that mankind may suffer due to the effects of progress in science. In the film, a medical advancement causes something much worse than the disease it cures. In an age where biological warfare is possible and great advances in science are common, the fear of an airborne virus is powerful. The film also shows the military blocking exits from New York. Each person is scanned for the virus, and those that fail the scan are not permitted to leave. A military quarantine would seem a real and frightening possibility in this situation. In recent times, people are more concerned about what a pandemic would mean for their lives and how the government would manage this type of crisis.

2. **Describe how Robert Neville takes some of the steps in the hero's journey as outlined by Campbell.**

Before the virus spread and killed most of the world's population, Neville elects to stay in the quarantined city and work on a cure. Even though his family wants Neville to leave with them, Neville stays. Neville starts his own adventure by volunteering to stay in the city and work on a cure, hoping he can find one before most of the world is infected. Destiny also chooses Neville by making him one the few who is immune. But even when Neville fears he is the only human left in the world, he continues to experiment on rats and zombies in the hope of finding a cure. He is separated from the rest of humanity, and has only his dog for company. His road of trials includes fighting zombies and capturing zombies and then testing possible cures on them. Anna acts in the role of goddess for Neville. She nourishes him with hope and faith. She believes that God has sent her to Neville and has faith that a survivors' colony exists. Neville says he doesn't believe that God has a plan, but Anna insists he can hear the plan if he listens. While trapped in his lab with the zombies attacking, Neville tries to reason with the creatures. He tells them he can save them, but they do not seem to care. It is then that Neville achieves illumination. He tells Anna that he can now hear God's plan. Neville gives Anna the cure for the virus and tells her to go to Vermont. Neville stays in his lab and kills the zombies and himself. However, he knows that his actions will save humanity.

3. **Explain the way the film is similar to the biblical flood story.**

Both the biblical flood story and *I Am Legend* are destruction myths. While the cause of the destruction is a manmade virus rather than a flood, the effects are similar. Neville implies that somehow man is responsible for the destruction of most of the population. Neville seem to be the only man left. While there is no express covenant between God and Neville, by the end of the film Neville feels that God is talking to him. Neville believes God's plan was for him to cure the virus and get it to the survivors. Neville accomplishes this. When Neville meets Anna, he explains how he was influenced by Bob Marley. He tells Anna that Marley though he could cure hate and racism by injecting love and music into people's lives. He says that Marley wanted to "light up the darkness." When Anna tells the story of Neville at the end of the film, she explains that he was a light in the darkness as he gave his life to restore humanity. While there is not actual rainbow, Neville's actions signal new beginning. Like the flood story, after destruction humanity goes on.

11. Into the Woods

Film Data

Year: 1991

Director: James Lapine

Length: 153 minutes

Rated: N/A

Characters/Actors

Bernadette Peters: The Witch

Chip Zien: Baker

Joanna Gleason: Baker's wife

Tom Aldredge: Narrator/Mysterious Man

Robert Westenberg: Wolf/Cinderella's Prince

Kim Crosby: Cinderella

Danielle Ferland: Little Red Riding Hood

Ben Wright: Jack

Barbara Bryne: Jack's mother

Pamela Winslow: Rapunzel

Connection to Chapters

Chapter 34. Applying Theory: How to Perform a Jungian Analysis

Chapter 37. Germany: Grimms' *Household Tales*

Recommended Scenes

The scene of the Witch telling the Baker how to reverse the curse occurs at 00:12:20.

The scene of Little Red Riding Hood and the wolf occurs at 00:18:24 through 00:21:12.

The scene of the Baker and his wife debating the morality of cheating Jack occurs at 00:25:02 through 00:26:05.

The scene of the princes singing about their dissatisfaction with marriage occurs at 01:34:31.

The scene of the Baker's wife and Cinderella's Prince having a tryst and then discussing it occurs at 01:48:42 through 01:56:12.

The scene of Little Red Riding Hood expressing reservations about killing the giant and Cinderella, the Baker, and Jack singing about the ambiguities of life of occurs at 02:15:35 through 02:20:23.

The scene of the resolution of the story occurs at 02:22:21 through the end of the film.

Instructor Viewing Information

Into the Woods is a filmed version of the Tony Award–winning Broadway musical. Stephen Sondheim wrote the music and lyrics. The book was written by James Lapine, and was inspired by Bruno Bettelheim's *Uses of Enchantment.* The musical's first act combines characters from the Grimms' tales and unifies their stories. The second act imagines what happens after fairy tales end. This is a musical for adults, featuring serious themes and much humor. Students should enjoy the sophisticated music, self-referential humor, and darker themes present in *Into the Woods.* This excellent musical should provide an enjoyable way to examine the household tales and their relevance for adult audiences.

Synopsis

Into the Woods follows familiar fairy tale characters Cinderella (Crosby), Jack (Wright), Little Red Riding Hood (Ferland), and others. Three characters invented for *Into the Woods,* the Baker (Zien) and his wife (Gleason) and an evil Witch (Peters), help tie the various other story lines together. A narrator (Aldredge) recounts and comments on the story. In Act I, the audience learns that the Baker and his wife want to have a child. They live next door to an evil witch who tells them that when the Baker was a boy, his father stole some beans from the witch's garden for the Baker's pregnant mother. The witch took the Baker's sibling and placed a curse on the Baker, making him unable to have children. The witch tells the Baker and his wife that she will reverse this curse and allow them to have a baby if they bring her certain items. The search for these items takes the couple on a journey that intersects with Little Red Riding Hood and her encounter with the Wolf (Westenberg), Jack and his adventures with a giant and a beanstalk, and Cinderella and her Prince (Westenberg). When Act I ends, the Baker's wife is pregnant, the witch is no longer a witch, and all of the other characters' problems are resolved happily. Act II imagines what might occur after the happy endings. A giant attacks the town, and the characters must work together to destroy it. Along the way, the characters examine what they really desire from life. Cinderella's Prince is unfaithful, the Baker's wife is killed by the giant, and other characters suffer losses. The group kills the giant together. Cinderella and the Baker raise his baby together, and they agree to take care of Jack and Little Red Riding Hood.

Discussion Questions

1. **Explain how the film reflects contemporary values.**

   The moral values of charity and self-sacrifice present in the film are both traditional and contemporary. The characters in *Into the Woods* also wrestle with the complexity of their moral choices. As in contemporary life, there are murky areas between good and bad, and the correct choice is not always clear. In the first act, Red Riding Hood sings that there is a difference between good and nice. This ambiguity is highlighted in the second act, as Cinderella and the Baker sing that giants and witches can be good and right. In the second act, the witch who kidnapped Rapunzel (Winslow) shows that she loves Rapunzel and is pained by her departure. The importance of parent/child bonds and the tension between a child leaving a parent to grow up are also important to contemporary audiences. The Baker examines the issue of a father's responsibility, from the point of view of being both a son and a father. The second half of *Into the Woods* explores the issue of wish fulfillment. The balancing of personal happiness with moral choices has resonance for contemporary audiences.

2. **Explain how the film is consistent with the Grimms' ideas of characters developing the moral values of charity and self-sacrifice.**

   At the start of the film, the characters only care about themselves. The Baker feels a few pangs of guilt about trading a few beans for Jack's cow, but his wife convinces him to make the deal. She reasons that if they really want a child, they have to do what is required. When the Baker says it is wrong to lie, she sings that the end justifies the means. Little Red Riding Hood and her grandmother kill the Wolf with a relish that seems unfeeling. In the second act, the characters begin to face the moral consequences of their choices. Jack's mother (Bryne) argues with the giant to protect Jack, and

44

eventually sacrifices her own life. Little Red Riding Hood argues that perhaps the group should show compassion toward the giant, and that killing is wrong. The Baker's wife protects her baby by leaving him with Red Riding Hood while she searches for the giant. When the Witch wants to give Jack to the giant in the hope that she will spare their lives, the others refuse. They all risk their lives to save Jack. At the end of the story, Jack and Red Riding Hood want to move in with the Baker. At first, he declines, saying his house is too small. But then he realizes he must help these children who lost their parents. Cinderella also agrees to help the Baker care for his child, Jack, and Red Riding Hood. When the story concludes, the characters realize they must help those in need and sacrifice for those they love. They have grown from selfish people to people who care about others.

3. **Describe the ways that the film, like the stories of the Grimm Brothers, is directed primarily at adults.**

While the fairy tale characters may be familiar to children, children would probably only be familiar with the sanitized versions of these tales, rather than the Grimms' grittier versions. Cinderella's stepsisters cut off their heels and toes to fit into Cinderella's slipper, Rapunzel is abandoned in a desert and gives birth to twins, and birds peck out the eyes of the mean stepsisters. The characters of the Baker and his wife, invented for *Into the Woods,* struggle with the very adult problem of infertility. Little Red Riding Hood and the Wolf suggest a sexual awakening. The princes reprise a song from the first act, this time expressing a desire for further conquests. To them, the chase is exciting and marriage leaves them bored. The Baker's wife and Cinderella's Prince tryst in the woods and face the moral consequences of adultery. Characters who are good people die in the second act, and those left behind grieve. The Baker must learn to live without his beloved wife, and Jack and Red Riding Hood must go on without their mothers and grandmother. The Baker faces the prospect of raising his child alone and is afraid, but he accepts responsibility. The issues that all of the characters must wrestle with are issues that are especially relevant to the lives of the adults. Throughout *Into the Woods,* all the characters examine what it means to be happy. The quest for personal happiness in a complex and changing world is an issue that continues to be an important one in the lives of most adults.

12. *Joseph Campbell and the Power of Myth,* Episode 1: "The Hero's Adventure"

Film Data

Year: 1988

Executive Producer: Joan Konner and Alvin H. Perlmutter

Length: 60 minutes

Rated: N/A (television mini-series)

Characters/Actors

Joseph Campbell: Himself

George Lucas: Himself

Bill Moyers: Himself/Interviewer

Connection to Chapters

Chapter 15. Theory: Joseph Campbell, *The Hero with a Thousand Faces* (Dave Whomsley)

Recommended Scenes

The scene of Bill Moyers introducing Joseph Campbell and the documentary occurs at 00:02:55 through 00:04:21.

The scene of Campbell discussing religious figures occurs at 00:11:54 through 00:14:55.

The scene of Campbell discussing *Star Wars* occurs at 00:17:17 through 00:24:01.

The scene of Campbell discussing the individual as a hero occurs at 00:27:00.

The scene of Campbell telling the Iroquois tale occurs at 00:28:42 through 00:34:14.

The scene of Campbell discussing dragons and inner desires occurs at 00:36:00 through 00:41:10.

Instructor Viewing Information

Joseph Campbell and the Power of Myth is a six-part documentary television mini-series. It consists of interviews of acclaimed scholar Joseph Campbell by Bill Moyers. The interviews were conducted in 1987 shortly before Campbell's death. Students will enjoy hearing an enthusiastic Campbell explain his ideas with vivid examples. Students will especially enjoy the discussion of the film *Star Wars* and the accompanying clips. A recommended special feature is a fifteen-minute segment of selections from the 2000 documentary *The Mythology of "Star Wars."* In these selections Bill Moyers interviews *Star Wars* writer/director George Lucas. Many students will be familiar with Lucas and his work, and even those who are not will especially enjoy hearing Lucas talk about Campbell's work. Episode 1, "The Hero's Adventure," is an excellent way to discuss Campbell's ideas about heroes.

Synopsis

Bill Moyers provides a brief introduction to Joseph Campbell and the series at the start of episode one. In episode 1, "The Hero's Adventure," Campbell discusses the motifs of the hero's adventures in many different cultures. Campbell talks about the religion and the hero's journey exemplified by Moses, Jesus, Buddha, and Mohammed. Moyers and Campbell also devote time to a discussion of the hero cycle in the film *Star Wars,* and they show and discuss specific clips from the film. Toward the end of this episode, Campbell relates the hero to present-day individuals. He uses the example of an Iroquois myth. Campbell and Moyers conclude by discussing the various cultural and psychological meaning of dragons, and the relevance of this for people today.

Discussion Questions

1. **Explain how Campbell uses religious figures to illustrate the hero's journey in the episode.**

   Campbell states that Moses, Jesus, Buddha, and Mohammed complete the hero's cycle of departure, fulfillment, and return. Furthermore, Campbell states that Moses is a hero because he ascends the mountain, meets with Yahweh, and returns with a tablet inscribed with rules for a whole new society. Campbell also states that both Jesus and Buddha resist three temptations, although they are not the same three temptations. Campbell further states that Jesus and Buddha both return and then choose disciples to help them teach what they learn. Campbell also states that Mohammed would go into a cave to meditate and then wrote the Koran.

2. **Describe how Campbell and Moyers use the film *Star Wars* to discuss the hero's journey in the episode.**

Campbell opines that the film *Star Wars* provides a perfect example of the hero cycle. He states that many of the old stories had the people entering unknown regions. In the film *Star Wars,* the characters venture into space, a place that is unknown. Campbell states that his provides "empty spaces for our imagination." Campbell also states that the film uses standard mythological figures. He cites the old man who helps the hero by giving him a weapon and psychological assistance as an example of this. Campbell also points to the scene in the film of the characters in the bar as a good example of the hero on the edge of an adventure. In the bar, Luke Skywalker meets several unusual characters, characters that have already been there and can tell tales about the places the hero intends to go. Campbell and Moyers discuss the scene in the film where the characters are trapped in a garbage compacter. Campbell points to this as an example of characters trapped in the belly of the whale. Campbell states that the belly of the whale is a trial the hero must face.

3. **Describe how Campbell contends in the episode that we are all heroes in our own lives.**

Campbell begins by discussing Rank's idea that, by virtue of surviving the birth process, we are all heroes. Moyers then asks Campbell if his ideas about heroes can help the individual. Campbell answers that each person should listen to their inner voices and resist committing to a system that is wrong, much like Luke Skywalker resists going to the dark side. Campbell states that you can become a hero by "following your bliss" and refusing to submit to a system that interferes with this. Campbell states that you should put yourself into situations that evoke your higher nature rather than your lower nature. Campbell concludes by saying that the adventure of being alive is one we should say yes to taking. He states that following your inner desires is a way of slaying dragons. Campbell tells Moyers that by following your bliss and going on your one hero journey, you are saving the world by saving yourself. He says that the influence of a vital person helps the world.

13. The Matrix

Film Data

Year: 1999

Director: The Wachowski Brothers

Length: 136 minutes

Rated: R

Characters/Actors

Keanu Reeves: Neo

Laurence Fishburne: Morpheus

Carrie-Anne Moss: Trinity

Hugo Weaving: Agent Smith

Gloria Foster: Oracle

Joe Pantoliano: Cypher

Connection to Chapters

Part IIA. Myths of Creation and Destruction—Creation: Introductory Overview

Chapter 5. The Bible: Genesis (Creation)

Chapter 15. Theory: Joseph Campbell, *The Hero with a Thousand Faces* (Dave Whomsley)

Chapter 33. Theory: C. G. Jung, *Man and His Symbols*

Recommended Scenes

The scene of Neo's first encounter with Agent Smith occurs at 00:17:09 through 00:21:50.

The scene of Morpheus offering Neo the choice of the red or blue pill and then freeing Neo occurs at 00:25:47 through 00:134:59.

The scene of Morpheus explaining the history of the matrix occurs at 00:41:28 through 00:46:29.

The scene of Neo visiting the oracle occurs at 01:14:30.

The scene of Neo rescuing Morpheus occurs at 01:41:06.

The scene of occurs Neo finally defeating Agent Smith occurs at 02:00:40 through 02:06:59.

Instructor Viewing Information

The Matrix is a science fiction action film. It was the first of a series of *Matrix* films. Students should be familiar with this film, but even those who are not will be able to understand the plot with little or no explanation. Students should enjoy the special effects, fast-paced plot, and exciting action sequences. *The Matrix* will provide an excellent catalyst for class discussion about Joseph Campbell's hero quest as well as many of C. J. Jung's idea. The film is also a good way to introduce the topic of creation myths.

Synopsis

Computer programmer and hacker Thomas/Neo (Reeves) has questions about his world. The legendary Morpheus (Fishburne) contacts Neo to arrange a meeting. After narrowly escaping police questioning, Trinity (Moss) and her crew bring Neo to Morpheus. Neo learns that the world as he knows it is a computer-generated program called the matrix. Artificial intelligence has created a dream world to control humans so the machines can use the body heat of humans as batteries. Humans are grown, not born, and they live in a dream state. Humans are connected by wires to machines. A small band of rebels lives on a ship in the real world. Morpheus believes a prophecy that says Neo is the one destined to save humanity from the matrix. Morpheus trains Neo, and Neo shows that he is the chosen one. The rebels are betrayed by fellow crew member Cypher (Pantoliano), and some of them are killed. Neo and Trinity fall in love. Neo is able to defeat his nemesis Agent Smith (Weaving) and other enemies inside the matrix. By the end of the film, Neo has embraced his destiny and returns to the matrix to continue his fight to free humanity.

1. **Describe how Neo takes the steps in the hero's journey as outlined by Campbell.**

   Neo's call to adventure is both active and passive. Neo is told that it is his destiny to be "the one." But Neo also chooses to go on the adventure when Morpheus offers him a choice of the red pill or the blue bill. Morpheus tells Neo that once he makes his choice, there is no turning back. Neo chooses to go on the journey and seek the truth. Morpheus acts as a protective figure for Neo both in and out of the matrix. He helps free Neo from his matrix cocoon. After Neo lands in a body of water, Morpheus and the rest of the crew help Neo aboard the ship. Neo has crossed the threshold. Neo travels to another world by leaving the dream world of the matrix to enter the real world. Once Neo enters the real world, Morpheus trains Neo to fight successfully in the matrix. Morpheus also takes Neo to meet the Oracle (Foster), who provides supernatural help to Neo. When Neo enters the real world, he attains an elevated state of consciousness. He knows the truth about the matrix, and he also learns how to bend the rules of the matrix to his advantage. Neo faces his true trials when he reenters the matrix after being trained by Morpheus. Here, he solves the riddle of the matrix and defeats the agents of the matrix. Neo takes the meeting with the goddess as a step in his relationship with Trinity. Trinity is a positive and nurturing force who believes in Neo's destiny. She also loves Neo; her love saves him from death near the end of the film. At the end of the film, Neo has become the master of both the real world and the world of the matrix. He chooses to use his newfound skills to help humanity. In the last scene of the film, a confident Neo reenters the matrix. He tells the machines running the matrix that he will show the people inside the matrix the truth, and he will show them a world where anything is possible.

2. **Explain how the story told by the film is a creation myth.**

   Morpheus explains to Neo that near the beginning of the twenty-first century, man invented artificial intelligence. Soon a conflict arose between man and a race of machines. The machines depended on solar power, so humans "scorched the sky." But the machines were able to use human body heat as a source of energy. The machines grew humans in fields and connected wires to the immobile humans. The machines created the matrix as an illusory world to control humans. Like early creation myths, this story is developed from an oral source. It serves to explain how humans came to be, the facts of the physical universe, and the meaning of human existence. Morpheus admits to Neo that he only possesses bits of information, implying that information may be added each time the story is told. Morpheus further explains that people talk of a man who lived at the time the matrix was first created. It was believed that this man could change the matrix at will and freed the first humans. This would explain how humans came to live outside the matrix. Morpheus explains that after this man died, an oracle prophesied that this man would return to help destroy the Matrix and free man. Morpheus believes that Neo is that man. This story provides a way for humans to believe that there is a better world yet to be created.

3. Explain how the film refers to the ideas of C. J. Jung.

When connected to the matrix, all of the humans are engaging in a type of dreaming. Morpheus even refers to the matrix as a "dream world." The characters in the film talk about having dreams that seem real and not being able to distinguish between dreams and reality. Through the matrix, all of the characters are sharing the same dream or the same view of the world. They see many of the same buildings and people and fight the same enemies. The idea of the collective unconscious is also shown through the tale of "the one" that is passed down by the characters both in and out of the matrix. Neo fits the description the archetypal hero/rescuer/redeemer that reappears miraculously after being devoured by a monster. No one in the film really knows the origin of the story, but all believe it. This refers to the Jung's idea that this hero or savior is an archetype that has always existed. All of the characters know about "the one," and it seems that the predecessors of these characters also knew this story. In the film, the characters believe that they have found the one in Neo (his name is an anagram for one). They believe that Neo will deliver them from oppression and save humanity.

14. Mighty Aphrodite

Film Data

Year: 1995

Director: Woody Allen

Length: 95 minutes

Rated: R

Characters/Actors

Lenny: Woody Allen

Leader: F. Murray Abraham

Amanda: Helena Bonham Carter

Kevin: Michael Rapaport

Linda Ash: Mira Sorvino

Laius: David Ogden Stiers

Tiresias: Jack Warden

Jocasta: Olympia Dukakis

Connection to Chapters

Chapter 21. Greece: Sophocles' *Oedipus the King*

Chapter 22. Theory: Claude Lévi-Strauss, *The Structural Study of Myth*

Recommended Scenes

The scene of the Leader refusing to help Lenny in his search occurs at 00:21:40.

The scene of the Greek Chorus warning Lenny about searching for his son's mother occurs at 00:18:12.

The scene of Jocasta, Laius, and the Greek Chorus talking about Oedipus occurs from 00:05:36 through 00:07:00.

The scene of the Greek Chorus talking about irony occurs at 01:28:00.

Instructor Viewing Information

Mighty Aphrodite is a comedy written by, directed by, and starring Woody Allen. The film tells the story of a modern New York couple who adopt a child and is interspersed with a Greek Chorus led by Leader (Abraham). The Greek Chorus uses characters from and speaks in the style of *Oedipus the King*. The Greek Chorus also mixes contemporary language and expression with some of the ideas in *Oedipus the King*. Students should enjoy the humor and wit throughout the film. The film provides an enjoyable and informative way to begin an examination of Oedipus, and provides a good start for a discussion of the role of the Greek Chorus and the concept of irony.

Synopsis

New York sportswriter Lenny (Allen) and his ambitious wife Amanda (Carter) adopt a son and name him Max. The couple soon experiences marital problems, but Lenny loves his smart and funny son. Lenny becomes obsessed with finding his son's biological mother. Throughout this film, a Greek Chorus, using some of the characters from *Oedipus,* narrates and comments on the story. Members of the Greek Chorus also interact with and advise Lenny. Lenny learns that his son's biological mother is Linda Ash (Sorvino), a porn star and prostitute who wishes to be an actress. He contacts Linda against the advice of the Chorus, and they become friends. Lenny helps Linda leave the prostitution business and introduces her to handsome boxer Kevin (Rapaport). Kevin and Linda date, but Kevin breaks off the relationship when he learns about Linda's past. Meanwhile, Tiresias (Warden) appears as a blind beggar and tells Lenny that his wife Amanda is having an affair. Lenny and Linda console each other by sleeping together. Lenny and Amanda realize they still love each other and reconcile. Linda leaves town and marries a pilot and has a child. The Greek Chorus tells us the child is Lenny's. Near the end of the film, Lenny, Linda, and their children run into each other in a department store. Both Lenny and Linda are happy with their lives, unaware that the other has their child. The film ends with the Leader of the Greek Chorus commenting on the irony of the situation, followed by a song and dance by the Greek Chorus.

Discussion Questions

1. **Explain the function of the Greek Chorus in the film.**

   Mighty Aphrodite uses the Greek Chorus in some traditional ways. The Greek Chorus talks among themselves and tells part of the story. The Greek Chorus also talks to Lenny, the film's the main character. When Lenny asks the Leader to help him in his search, the Leader replies that he cannot. Lenny tells the Lead that this is why he will always be a Chorus member, because, "You don't do anything, I act." The Greek Chorus warns Lenny to resist his impulse to find his son's biological mother. When doing so, they say, "O cursed fate, certain thoughts are better left unthunk." The Leader tells Lenny that it is curiosity that kills people, not the ozone layer. Throughout the film, the Greek Chorus speaks in unison, mixing the style of the Greek Chorus in *Oedipus* with contemporary informal language.

2. **Describe how the film refers to Freud's use of *Oedipus*.**

   The film begins with the Greek Chorus introducing the characters of Laius (Stiers) and Jocasta (Dukakis). Laius extols the virtues of his son Oedipus and then explains humorously that Oedipus killed him and "ran off with my wife." Jocasta further explains the story, ending with the fact that Oedipus accidentally killed her husband and then shared a bed with her, not knowing that she was his mother. A member of the Chorus responds by saying that then "a whole profession was born, charging sometimes two hundred dollars an hour, and a fifty minute hour at that." The scene ends with Jocasta and the rest of the Greek Chorus discussing the ramifications of Lenny wanting a child and relating these desires to the story of Oedipus.

3. **Describe how the film shows the overvaluing of blood relations.**

   In the film, Lenny is obsessed with meeting his son's biological mother, assuming his son's wonderful traits were inherited. He ignores the warnings of the Greek Chorus, and takes risks to find Linda. Lenny is undeterred when he learns the truth about Linda, and tries to help her improve her life. He overvalues her biological connection to his adopted son Max, thinking that meeting Linda will make his life more satisfying. He even has a brief affair with Linda near the end of the film.

4. **Describe how irony is used in the film.**

Linda and Lenny spend a lot of time together, but he never tells her that his adopted son Max is her biological son. She even sees a picture of Max and does not learn the truth. At the end of *Mighty Aphrodite,* Lenny and Linda and their children meet. Each looks at the other's child and is unaware of the truth. Despite keeping the truth from Linda, Lenny never learns that Linda has his biological child. The Leader of the Greek Chorus tells the audience the truth and the Greek Chorus comments that life is ironic.

15. Oedipus Rex

Film Data

Year: 1967

Director: Pier Paolo Pasolini

Length: 104 minutes

Rated: N/A

Characters/Actors

Jocasta: Silvana Mangano

Oedipus: Franco Citti

Merope: Alida Valli

Creon: Carmelo Bene

Tiresias: Julian Beck

Laius: Luciano Bartoli

Connection to Chapters

Chapter 21. Greece: Sophocles, *Oedipus the King*

Chapter 22. Theory: Claude Lévi-Strauss, *The Structural Study of Myth*

Recommended Scenes

The scene in Fascist Italy occurs from the start of the film through 00:11:57.

The scene of Oedipus cheating at his discus match occurs at 00:18:01.

The scene of the laughing oracle telling Oedipus his fate occurs at 00:35:32.

The scene of Oedipus fighting and killing Laius and his men occurs from 00:35:25 through 00:43:41.

The scene of Oedipus talking to and killing the sphinx occurs from 00:49:22 through 00:50:38.

The scene of Oedipus and Jocasta sleeping together for the first time occurs at 00:54:32.

The scene of Tiresias telling Oedipus the truth occurs from 01:08:13 through 01:14:31.

The scene of Oedipus and Jocasta discussing the truth occurs from 01:25:34 through 01:28:59.

The scene of Oedipus discovering Jocasta dead and blinding himself occurs at 01:36:14.

Instructor Viewing Information

Oedipus Rex is written and directed by acclaimed filmmaker Pier Paolo Pasolini, and is based on the play by Sophocles. There are modern scenes of Fascist Italy at the start of the film and scenes of then-contemporary Italy at the end of the film. The bulk of the film in between tells a version of *Oedipus Rex*. This section of *Oedipus Rex* was filmed in Morocco. Students who are interested in film may be familiar with Pasolini's work, but knowledge of the filmmaker is not needed to appreciate the film. Although the film is in Italian with English subtitles, the dialogue is spare, so reading the subtitles should not be onerous for students. The visual aspects of the film are most compelling and students should appreciate the scenery and costumes. The film is a good companion piece to the play by Sophocles, and comparison and contrast of the two works should start an engaging discussion about the themes of the play. The film's use of visual techniques and the modern sections of the film should make a fine starting point for a discussion of Freud's ideas inspired by this myth.

Synopsis

Oedipus Rex begins with a short segment in twentieth-century Fascist Italy. A mother cares for her newborn son while the baby's father, a soldier in uniform, feels jealous of his son. The scene then shifts to a barren desert, where a man leaves an infant on the ground. A shepherd finds the baby and gives him to a childless king and queen. Oedipus (Citti) grows up and is haunted by bad dreams. He visits the oracle to ask their meaning. The oracle laughs at Oedipus and reveals that his fate is to kill his father and make love with his mother. In an attempt to escape his fate, Oedipus wanders the desert toward Thebes. He encounters a group of men who order him to leave the road. Chases and fights ensue, and Oedipus kills all but one of them. Oedipus then kills the sphinx, thought to be the cause of the troubles plaguing Thebes. Oedipus is rewarded with marriage to Queen Jocasta (Mangano) and becomes King. After this, the title "Part Two" appears on the screen. This section of the film opens with a crying baby in the desert, surrounded by corpses. King Oedipus is asked to find the cause of a terrible plague afflicting Thebes. Oedipus searches for the man who murdered the former King, Laius (Bartoli). Blind Tiresias (Beck) tells Oedipus the truth. Oedipus does not want to believe that he has killed his father, married his mother, and caused the plague. Jocasta realizes the truth and hangs herself. Oedipus sees Jocasta dead and pokes out his eyes. He wanders blind, playing a flute. The film ends with blind Oedipus playing a flute in present-day Italy. Oedipus is led through the city to a meadow where the infants in the film were held. Oedipus proclaims, "Life ends where it begins."

Discussion Questions

1. **Describe the film's view of fate and free will in the life of Oedipus.**

The film adds some scenes not present in the play and emphasizes other scenes in the play, which point to Oedipus' personality and choices as responsible for his fate. The film shows a young Oedipus cheating in a discus match and then fighting with the players when he is accused of cheating. While Laius and his men start an altercation with Oedipus on the road, the fight and chase sequence that follows is violent and emotional. Oedipus, upset after hearing the oracle's prophecy, kills Laius and his men with relish. Citti, in the role of Oedipus, is contemporary looking and pugilistic. He is defiant during the discus match, the fight, the search for Laius' murderer, and his discovery of the truth. He denies that he killed his father and married his mother just as he denied cheating in the discus match. Before Oedipus kills the sphinx, the creature begins to tell him about the abyss inside Oedipus. Oedipus states that he does not want to hear about it. The film seems to suggest that Oedipus' refusal to grow and to change lead to his inability to see the truth about himself and, thus, to his eventual destruction. At the end of the film, Oedipus states, "There, now all is clear, willed, not imposed by destiny."

2. **Describe how the film refers to Freud's theories about *Oedipus*.**

The film's initial eleven-minute sequence in Fascist Italy makes some overt points about Freud's theories. The infant's father resents the attention his wife gives the baby. He even looks at the baby and states, "You are here to take my place . . . send me again into the void and rob me of all I have." At the end of the sequence, the father sleeps with his wife and then goes into the baby's room and grabs him by the ankles. The scene then shifts to the desert, where a bound baby Oedipus is left. When Oedipus marries Jocasta, we see that their relationship is both passionate and loving. Their love scenes are rather erotic, as Oedipus strokes Jocasta's face and calls her "my love." Even after Tiresias suggests that Oedipus murdered Laius, Jocasta and Oedipus sleep together after Jocasta wonders aloud about how many men have slept with their mother in their dreams. When Oedipus finally faces the truth, he screams at Jocasta, calls her mother, and attempts to have sex with her. When Oedipus sees that Jocasta killed herself, Jocasta is partially nude. This serves to emphasize their sexual connection. When Oedipus screams and blinds himself, his grief seems to be for Jocasta his wife and lover, rather than Jocasta his mother.

3. **Explain how the film differs in significant ways from the play *Oedipus the King*.**

The film bookends the ancient story with a contemporary sequence at the beginning and at the end of the film. Both scenes emphasize the theme of *Oedipus the King*. Most of the film is shot in the Moroccan desert. The costumes look like pieces of twigs, trees, and objects found on the ground. The costumes and arid landscape suggest a prehistoric time. This is quite a contrast with the modern sequences and seems to suggest this myth belongs in some ways to all time periods, yet its themes are rather primal. The Greek Chorus in the play is not present in the film. The plot unfolds both visually and through dialogue between the characters. Close shots of the actors emphasize the emotion and relationships between the characters. The sphinx Oedipus encounters is a strange-looking human. Instead of solving a riddle, Oedipus kills the sphinx. This emphasizes a war with his inner demons rather than the use of his intellect.

16. Opera Jawa (Requiem from Java)

Film Data

Year: 2006

Director: Garin Nugroho

Length: 120 minutes

Rated: N/A

Characters/Actors

Martinus Miroto: Setio

Eko Supriyanto: Ludiro

Artika Sari Devi: Siti

Retno Maruti: Sukesi

Jecko Siompo Pui: Anom

Connection to Chapters

Chapter 18. India: The *Ramayana*

Recommended Scenes

The scene of Seito singing to Siti about faithfulness occurs at 00:44:32.

The scene of Ludiro's mother extolling Siti's goodness occurs at 00:20:13 through 00:21:23.

The scene of Seito rejecting Siti occurs at 00:33:43.

The scene of Siti and Ludiro dancing on Ludiro's bed occurs at 00:44:12 through 00:47:30.

The scene of Siti again going to Ludiro occurs at 01:08:19 through 01:15:59.

The scene of the dancers singing about Sinta and Ram occurs at 01:29:29.

The scene of Seito killing Siti occurs at 01:41:59.

Instructor Viewing Information

The film begins with a text stating that it is a version of the abduction of Sita (referred to in this film as Sinta), often dramatized by Javanese dance and puppetry. This contemporary retelling imagines that both men love Sinta, and focuses on Sinta's conflict and purity. The film is in Indonesian with English subtitles, but almost all of the words are sung, and much of the story is told through movement, so students should not be daunted by the subtitles. Many students may be unfamiliar with both the place and the format used to tell the story, so some context may be needed. But students should enjoy the visually and aurally lush film. *Opera Jawa* is an excellent way to discuss the *Ramayana* and its cultural importance today.

Synopsis

Siti (Devi) and her husband Setio (Miroto) appear happy and in love. Siti used to dance the role of Sinta, but now Siti and Sieto farm and make pottery, and they struggle to get by. Ludiro (Supriyanto), a wealthy butcher, also loves Siti and pursues her while her husband is away selling his wares. Siti is nostalgic for her life as a dancer and is tempted by the wealthy and exciting Ludiro. She feels guilty about her fantasies, and bemoans her inability to tell right from wrong. Siti and Ludiro participate in a group dance. When Sieto returns from his trip, he seems suspicious and rejects Siti's embraces. When Setio leaves again, Siti follows a trail of candles to Ludiro's bed. In a scene involving shadows, song, and dance, Siti and Ludiro share a passionate encounter. She expresses guilt over her attraction and runs away. When Sieto returns, he finds Siti gone and wonders if love and fidelity are also gone. An anguished Seito uses clay and puppets in a bizarre performance ritual to express his feelings. While this is happening, the economic conditions in the village worsen, and protesters demonstrate against poverty and their exploitation by the rich. There are news reports of escalating violence. Unable to forget Siti, Ludiro lures her to him with a long red dance scarf. Siti goes to Ludiro, but again returns to her husband. However, now their relationship is damaged. Sieto joins the protesters. Ludiro is killed. Sita sings about the joys of being a woman. Siti and Seito embrace on the beach. Seito then kills Siti and tears out her heart. The film ends with a radio news station report on the arrest of Sieto for the murders of Siti and Ludiro.

Discussion Questions

1. **Describe how the characters in the film illustrate the concept of *dharma*.**

Throughout the film, the characters sing about the importance of faithfulness. Ludiro's mother states that her son loves Siti, a woman who used to dance the role of Sinta. She explains that Siti no longer dances "out of respect to her husband" and because she is faithful. The value of all types of faithfulness in a marriage is emphasized here. Even when Siti is tempted by Ludiro, she worries about her inability to tell right from wrong. Siti recognizes the concept of moral behavior. Even when Siti and Ludiro dance on Ludiro's bed, Siti worries about the spiritual consequences of adultery. She wonders what will become of her if she betrays her husband. The film also uses the political conflict in the story to highlight the moral and immoral behavior of the characters. Ludiro is a wealthy butcher who may be using gangs to rob the poor. He is aligned with those exploiting the poor. The film shows questionable moral behavior in his personal life and in his business life. Seito and Siti are married and aligned with the oppressed poor. By the end of the film, Seito (who appears to have behaved morally in his marriage) joins the protesters. But Seito is jailed at the end of the film for the murder of his wife and for the murder of Ludiro. Text appearing at the end of the film dedicates the film to victims of violence. Despite the fact that he may have been wronged in his marriage, Seito's violent behavior was immoral and was punished.

2. **Explain how the film shows the importance of the *Ramayana* in the lives of these contemporary characters.**

Through the film, several characters mention the story of Sinta/Sita and Rama. In the beginning of the film, Seito compares his life with Siti to the story of Sinta and Rama. He sings that when Sinta and Rama were banished, all they had left was their faithfulness to each other. Seito says that now that their land is barren and Siti and Seito struggle to make a living, all they have is their faithfulness. Seito and Siti are happy in their marriage, despite the economic hardships they face. They place a high value on their marriage and seem inspired by the ancient tale. However, like Rama, Seito begins to doubt Siti's fidelity, without any actual proof of betrayal. Like Rama, he initially rejects Siti and allows his doubt to destroy their marriage. Like Sinta being lured by a deer, Siti is lured by a red dance scarf. Near the end of the film, we see a traditional performance. The dancers sing about the fallow earth and present times. They sing that like Rama and Sinta, who "no longer recognized their world," what remains is hope, love, and faithfulness. Through the song, the film shows scenes of Ludiro and Sieto. The world of these characters has changed in many ways. Changing economic times forced Seito to stop performing and then to stop farming and making pottery. The changing rules of his marriage leave him alone. The climate of violence and poverty changes the village to a place in which neither man can live. Like the characters in the myth, the characters in the film must face a new reality.

3. **Describe how the film incorporates ancient traditions surrounding the myth.**

The film begins with an obese man singing the story of Rama and Sinta with much humor. The performer acknowledges the many different versions of the story by explaining that although everyone wants to know what happened in this ancient story, no two people ever agree on the whole truth and everyone thinks that their version is the correct one. This may also help explain the many changes in this modern retelling. This film uses music, dance, puppets, masks, and lush scenery to enhance the splendor of the tale, using traditional elements in new ways. The effect is beautiful and vibrant and elevates the story to an almost magical realm. But as in the traditional tale, the characters' problems are very human dilemmas. The filmmakers enhance this idea by also telling a gritty and violent political tale, while still using the same techniques that emphasize the grandeur of the story. These techniques allow the characters to act in ways that seem beyond human possibility, but also emphasize the pain of their very human struggles, and their relevance today.

17. Pan's Labyrinth (El laberinto del fauno)

Film Data

Year: 2006

Director: Guillermo del Toro

Length: 119 minutes

Rated: R

Characters/Actors

Ivana Baquero: Ofelia

Sergi López: Vidal

Maribel Verdú: Mercedes

Doug Jones: Fauno/Pale Man

Ariadna Gil: Carmen

Álex Angulo: Doctor

Connection to Chapters

Chapter 15. Theory: Joseph Campbell, *The Hero with a Thousand Faces* (Dave Whomsley)

Chapter 33. Theory: C. G. Jung, *Man and His Symbols*

Chapter 37. Germany: Grimms' *Household Tales*

Chapter 42. *Harry Potter*: A Rankian Analysis of the Hero of Hogwarts

Recommended Scenes

The scene of Ofelia's initial encounter with the fairy and faun occurs at 00:21:00 through 00:26:00.

The scene of Ofelia battling the toad occurs at 00:35:00 through 00:39:00.

The scene of Ofelia encountering the Pale Man and eating grapes begins at 00:54:00.

The scene of the angry faun telling Ofelia that she broke the rules occurs at 01:19:00.

The scene of the doctor disobeying Vidal and then being shot occurs at 01:25:00.

The scene of the faun giving Ofelia one last chance and the resolution of the story occurs at 01:38:10 through the end of the film,

Instructor Viewing Information

Pan's Labyrinth is the work of respected Mexican filmmaker Guillermo del Toro. The film is in Spanish with English subtitles. *Pan's Labyrinth* begins with the recitation of a fairy tale. This sets the stage for the two stories in this film. The story of Ofelia and her encounters with the faun in the labyrinth contains many elements present in the Grimm Brothers' fairy tales. The second story also involves Ofelia and the aftermath of World War II. This second story is harrowing and serious, yet both stories share some common features. *Pan's Labyrinth* is an excellent example of a fairy tale directed at adults. It is visually stunning and the plot is engrossing. Students will enjoy the original effects and involving story, and should not be put off by the subtitles. The film should provide an excellent way to examine the ideas of Joseph Campbell and Otto Rank about heroes and Jung's theories about the unconscious, as well as providing a good way to discuss household tales.

Synopsis

Pan's Labyrinth takes place in 1944 Spain. Cruel and vicious Captain Vidal (López) hunts the anti-Franco rebels hiding in the woods. Vidal's wife Carmen (Gil) is pregnant with their child and Carmen and Carmen's daughter Ofelia (Baquero) move to the Captain's house. Vidal treats both of them with disdain, seeming to only care for his unborn child. Ofelia has an encounter with a fairy that at first appears to be a praying mantis. The fairy takes her to a creature called a faun (Jones) who looks like a cross between a human, a goat, and a large malevolent elf. The faun tells Ofelia that she is really a princess from a magical kingdom and must complete three tasks in order to return there. While Ofelia attempts to complete the tasks, life continues to grow more difficult in Vidal's house. Vidal shoots and tortures rebels and Carmen grows ill. Vidal's maid Mercedes (Verdú) befriends Ofelia, and Ofelia learns that Mercedes is secretly helping the rebels. Ofelia keeps this secret. Carmen's condition worsens and she dies after giving birth to a son. Mercedes is caught by the Captain, but escapes. The faun tells Ofelia that her last chance to return to the kingdom is to bring her brother to the labyrinth. She does so, but when she learns that a few drops of her brother's innocent blood is necessary to open the portal to the kingdom, she refuses to hurt her brother. Vidal discovers her, takes the baby, and shoots Ofelia. Carmen and the rebels take the baby to raise and kill Vidal. The film ends with Ofelia dying in the labyrinth, and then making a spiritual return to her kingdom. We are told that she ruled wisely for many centuries and was loved by her people.

Discussion Questions

1. **Explain how the film illustrates the maturation and initiation cycle, as well as Rank's ideas of the family romance.**

   According to the fairy tale introduction, Ofelia's "real" parents are the king and queen of a magical kingdom. Thus, Ofelia is separated from her natural mother and father. But even if this were not the case, Ofelia's biological father is dead, and she now lives with her cruel stepfather and well-meaning but weak mother. Her substitute father mistreats her. Ofelia journeys to a magical place in the labyrinth and the faun gives her three tasks to complete. Ofelia goes under a tree to get a key inside a toad and places a healing mandrake root under her mother's bed. During her last task, she is warned that she will see a sumptuous feast, but she must not eat or drink anything. Ofelia disobeys and eats two grapes. The angry faun tells her she broke the rules and can never return to the kingdom. The faun gives her one last chance to return to the kingdom. Ofelia refuses to hurt her brother. At the end of the film, she learns that the last task was to choose to spill her own blood, rather than shed innocent blood. Ofelia passes the test and is reunited with her royal parents. Her true identity has been proven, and she assumes her rightful place as princess.

2. **Describe how Ofelia takes the steps in the hero's journey as outlined by Campbell.**

   In synthesizing the ideas of both Otto Rank and Carl Jung, Campbell emphasized the importance of both male and female figures in the hero's adventure. Although Campbell's analysis envisioned a male hero, it is instructive to examine the way contemporary female hero figures may follow some of these same patterns. Ofelia eagerly answers the call to adventure after meeting the fairy and the faun. At the instruction of the faun, she undertakes three tasks. The faun gives her supernatural aid by providing a book with blank pages where instructions appear, chalk that can create a door, and a magical root that heals her mother. The faun also sends the fairies with Ofelia to help her fight danger along the way. Campbell bases his ideas on a gendered, Freudian model: the male hero fights a (same-sex) father figure and resists a(n) (opposite-sex) temptress and unites with a(n) (opposite-sex) goddess. It would stand to reason that these genders would be reversed if the hero is female. However, Ofelia seems to inherit the characteristics of a male hero, as her main struggle is with her fascist stepfather Vidal, and her main inspiration is the spy Mercedes. The faun, however, is both Ofelia's helper and her tempter, and his gender is reversed from the Campbell model. It would seem that del Toro has interwoven different approaches to this mythological quest. During the first task, Ofelia must go underneath a tree to retrieve a key from the inside of a giant toad. This small underground space where Ofelia encounters the toad very much resembles the belly of the whale. The toad regurgitates itself and Ofelia recovers the key. During the last trial, Ofelia gives into the temptation of the grapes, and it appears she has failed. However, Ofelia proves herself worthy at the end of her adventure. She resists the temptation of returning to her kingdom and refuses to give the faun her baby brother. Although Ofelia dies, she reaches a new understanding of her place in the world. She is now a princess, reunited with her royal parents.

3. **Describe the ways that the film, like the stories of the Grimm Brothers, is directed primarily at adults.**

The film uses the language of fairy tales at both the start and the end. When we first see Ofelia, she is reading a book of fairy tales. But the fairy tale that Ofelia enters is quite different than contemporary sanitized version of these tales, and is closer to the darker Grimm Brothers' tales. We can also see parallels with the adult war story in the film. While Ofelia refuses to hurt her brother, she also keeps the secret of Mercedes helping the rebels. Ofelia stands up to the faun and risks her life to save her brother. Mercedes risks her life to save her own brother and the rest of the rebels. The faun asks Ofelia to follow his last order without question. This is similar to the doctor (Angulo) who has been helping the rebels, refusing to obey the evil Vidal. Against Vidal's orders, the doctor mercifully kills the rebel being tortured by Vidal. The doctor tells Vidal that he cannot obey just for the sake of obeying. Vidal then shoots and kills the doctor. The adult themes of fighting evil and sacrificing your life to save an innocent life are present in both stories. Ofelia encounters the frightening monster the Pale Man and narrowly escapes with her life. Vidal does not look as frightening as the Pale Man, but appears even more evil.

4. **Describe the ways that the film refers to Jung's ideas about individuation and Rank's ideas about heroes.**

Fairy tales and myths often describe the start of this process with a king who has grown old or fallen ill. In Ofelia's case, her biological father has died. When she returns to her kingdom, her father the king looks quite old. The queen tells Ofelia that she has been waiting for her for a long time. Mazes and passages were thought to represent the unknown or unconscious. At the start of the film, Ofelia is warned that it is easy to get lost in the labyrinth. It has many twists, but Ofelia always finds her way. Much like Harry Potter, Ofelia is the child of royal and perhaps immortal parents. Ofelia is separated from her royal parents, and death takes away both of her mortal parents. Ofelia is helped by an underling, Vidal's servant Mercedes. Although Mercedes does not succeed in preventing Ofelia's death at the hands of Vidal, Mercedes does save Ofelia's baby brother from life with Vidal. When Ofelia questions the faun's initial claim that she is Princess Moanna, the faun tells Ofelia that she bears a mark on her shoulder. Much like Harry Potter, Ofelia bears a mark that proves her status. By the end of the film, Ofelia achieves reconciliation with her father the king.

18. Popol Vuh: The Creation Myth of the Maya

Film Data

Year: 1988

Director: Patricia Amlin

Length: 60 minutes

Rated: N/A

Characters/Actors

Larry George, Yakima Nation: Narrator

Hun Ah Pu: Hunter

X Balan Ke: Jaguar Deer

Connection to Chapters

Chapter 11. Mesoamerica: *Popol Vuh*

Recommended Scenes

The scene of the creators trying to make intelligent beings occurs at 00:04:45 through 00:06:22 of Part 1.

The scene of the twins talking to the rat and learning about their destiny occurs at 00:07:17 of Part 3.

The scene of the twins planting stalks of corn for their mother and grandmother occurs at 00:05:55 of Part 4.

The scenes of the twins' feats in the underworld occur at 00:00:45 of Part 5 through 00:05:22 of Part 6.

The scenes of the death of the twins, the beggars defeating the lords of the underworld, and the resolution of the story occur at 00:06:26 of Part 6 through 00:03:54 of Part 7.

Instructor Viewing Information

Popol Vuh: The Creation Myth of the Maya is an animated film that tells the story of the *Popol Vuh*. According to a note at the beginning of the film, the drawings used for the animation are taken directly from classic Maya pottery. The film is available on YouTube (http://theinnkeeperstail.blogspot.com/search?q=popol+vuh) in seven parts. A narrator tells the story, and occasionally the characters use dialogue. The film starts with the creation of humanity and then tells the story of the birth of the Hero Twins and their adventures. Students should enjoy the clear and enjoyable way these tales are portrayed. The film is an enjoyable and interesting way to introduce the *Popol Vuh*.

Synopsis

Part 1 tells the story of Grandmother of Day and Light attempting to create intelligent beings to worship their creators. After creating and destroying beings of mud and wood, humans are created. Then the story of the Hero Twins, Hunter and Jaguar Deer, begins. Part 2 tells about the fathers of the twins, two brothers who were artists and magicians, as well as ball players. The brothers are invited to play ball in the underworld, but they are tricked and killed by the lords of the underworld. The rest of Part 2 recounts the story of Little Blood, a young virgin who becomes pregnant with the sons of the dead brothers. The pregnant girl defeats the lords of the underworld when they try to kill her. She climbs to earth to meet her children's grandmother, who initially doubts her story. The Hero Twins are born and grow up in Part 3. They learn their destiny is to be ballplayers like their fathers. In Part 4, the twins play ball using the equipment belonging to their fathers. Like their fathers, the twins are invited to play ball in the underworld. In Part 5, the twins arrive in the underworld and refuse to be tricked as their fathers were. They outwit the lords of the underworld and pass a series of tests. In Part 6, the twins see a vision of their own deaths. The twins arrange for a seer to tell the lords that when the twins die, the lords should chop up their bones and scatter them in the ocean. The twins then jump into a fire and are killed. Their bones are scattered. In Part 7, two beggars appear and begin doing magical feats. They are invited to the underworld. The beggars kill all of the lords in the underworld, and then reveal that they are the Hero Twins and have avenged their fathers' deaths. After the twins defeat all in the underworld forever, the twins walk into the sky and become the sun and the moon.

Discussion Questions

1. **Describe how the film portrays the view the creators had of early man.**

   The film shows the grandmother and grandfather creator being asked to make beings who would be respectful, obedient, and intelligent. The creators wanted beings able to praise their makers. The film states that the first beings were made from mud and earth. But these beings could not speak intelligibly nor could they multiply. They were destroyed. The next beings were carved from wood. These beings had no hearts or minds. They also did not think of their makers. Additionally, they abused the trees, rocks, and their dogs. Their dogs, the trees, and the rocks attacked these beings and they were destroyed. The god Heart of Sky caused a great flood and those that escaped became the monkeys. The gods wanted beings who would praise them, so when their creations could not do so, they were destroyed. However, beings were destroyed not only because they could not or would not praise their creators, but because they had no hearts. The abusive way the wood beings treated their animals and environment seems just as important to the creators.

2. **Explain how the film portrays the significance of corn.**

   In the beginning of the film, the narrator introduces the creation story by mentioning the birth of the sun and moon and the sowing of the first corn. When the twins' grandmother does not believe Little Blood is telling the truth, she gives her a test. Little Blood must gather corn from the fields. She gets divine help and is able to pass the test. When the twins are called to play ball in the underworld, they comfort their mother and grandmother by planting corn stalks in the middle of their houses. The twins explain that if the corn stalk dries up, it means that they are dead, but if it grows, the twins are alive. When the twins die in the fire, the corn stalks shrivel up. The narrator explains that the twins' death is like a seed that must die before it is born. The film shows the corn to be much more than just an important food source. The corn is an important symbol in the life cycle here. Before the twins are born, their mother uses corn to pass a test and prove that lineage of her unborn babies. The adult twins use corn to tell of their deaths.

3. **Describe the cultural insights provided in the film's portrayal of the achievements of the twins.**

   The stories of the twins' feats show the value placed on playing ball, cleverness, magic, and trickery. Skill at ball playing is important to the fathers of the twins, who play so well they are invited to the underworld, where they are eventually killed. The narrator tells us that the twins reward the rat for telling them that their destiny is to be ball players. The twins are happy that they are supposed to play ball, not farm. But playing ball here is more than just a game; it can be dangerous. Those skilled in this sport receive invitations to visit the underworld. When the twins arrive in the underworld, the narrator points out that the twins were not tricked like their fathers were tricked. The twins use their cleverness to escape death in the underworld on numerous occasions. They use their magic to persuade insects and animals to help them. They persuade mosquitoes to bite all of the lords in the underworld so that the twins may learn all of their names. The twins use fireflies to make their cigars appear to be lit, so they can trick the lords and pass the test. They promise knives that those knives will have animals for the rest of their existence in exchange for the knives sparing their lives. After their deaths, the twins return as magical beggars who again trick the lords of the underworld and finally destroy them. The twins show the importance of avenging their fathers' deaths. They use magic again, but for honorable purposes. When they have destroyed the evil lords and avenged the deaths of their fathers, the twins light up the world by becoming the sun and moon.

19. Red Riding Hood

Film Data

Year: 2011

Director: Catherine Hardwicke

Length: 100 minutes

Rated: PG-13

Characters/Actors

Valerie: Amanda Seyfried

Solomon: Gary Oldman

Cesaire: Billy Burke

Peter: Shiloh Fernandez

Henry: Max Irons

Suzette: Virginia Madsen

Grandmother: Julie Christie

Connection to Chapters

Chapter 34. Applying Theory: How to Perform a Jungian Analysis

Chapter 37. Germany: Grimms' *Household Tales*

Recommended Scenes

The scene of Valerie talking about being a good girl and encountering Peter occurs at 00:4:10.

The scene of Peter and Valerie embracing before being interrupted occurs at 00:39:00 through 00:40:08.

The scene of the wolf speaking to Valerie for the first time occurs at 00:44:15.

The scene of Valerie suspecting her grandmother of being the wolf occurs at 01:19:02.

The scene of Valerie confronting her father, killing the wolf, and changing her life occurs from 01:24:20 through the end of the film.

Instructor Viewing Information

Red Riding Hood is loosely based on the Grimm Brothers' *Little Red Cap*. The film is directed by Catherine Hardwicke, who directed the first *Twilight* film. Students may also recognize actor Billy Burke, who played Bella's father in the *Twilight* series. Students may notice some similarities between the two films, and that should be a nice way to open the discussion. Although students may find the film a bit plodding and some of the plot points contrived, they should enjoy some aspects of this version of the fairy tale. *Red Riding Hood* should provide a good starting point to a discussion of household tales and Jungian analysis of household tales.

Synopsis

Valerie (Seyfried) lives in the small village of at an unspecified time in the past, and wears a red cape made for her by her grandmother. Valerie and woodcutter Peter (Fernandez) are in love, but Valerie's parents have arranged for her to marry the wealthier Henry (Irons). The village has an uneasy truce with a werewolf, sacrificing a pig every full moon so the villagers' lives are spared. But the twenty-year-old truce is broken when the wolf kills Valerie's older sister. When the villagers, led by Valerie's father Cesaire (Burke), fail to find the wolf, werewolf expert Father Solomon (Oldman) is called to help. He determines that the werewolf is a member of the village. Valerie suspects Henry, Peter, and even her own grandmother (Christie). The wolf returns, terrorizes the villagers, and corners Valerie and her friend. The wolf speaks to Valerie and calls her by name, telling her that she and the wolf are the same. He says he will return for her. But when Father Solomon learns that Valerie spoke to the wolf, he accuses her of being a witch and jails her, intending to sacrifice her to the wolf. Max and Peter plan to rescue Valerie, but Valerie believes either man could be the wolf. The wolf appears again and asks Valerie to come with him. Valerie escapes and goes to her grandmother's house and finds her grandmother has been killed by the werewolf. Valerie encounters her father, Cesaire, and learns that he is the werewolf. He wants to make Valerie an invincible werewolf like him, but she does not want to be a killer. Peter breaks in to the cabin and fights with Cesaire, but Valerie kills her father the wolf. Valerie and Peter sew rocks into Cesaire's belly and throw his body into the lake. Despite the fact that the wolf has bitten Peter and he will turn into a werewolf at the full moon, Valerie refuses to kill Peter. Peter runs away to learn to control his wolf nature, after consummating his relationship with Valerie. Valerie leaves the village and goes to the forest to wait for Peter's return. When he returns to her as a wolf, she smiles.

Discussion Questions

1. **Explain how the film reflects both traditional and contemporary values.**

   In a voiceover at the beginning of the film, Valerie discusses her mother's warnings about not breaking the rules, not talking to strangers, and being a good girl. Like some fairy tales, the traditional values of sexual purity for women and fidelity are emphasized here. Although Valerie engages in sexual behavior with Peter, they are interrupted before they consummate their relationship. When Valerie's father learns of his wife Suzette's (Madsen) infidelity, the wolf kills her former lover and injures Suzette. Upon learning that Valerie's sister is the product of that affair and not his biological daughter, he accidentally kills her in anger. The contemporary values of individuality and female independence are also present here. Father Solomon and the villagers persecute Valerie for being different, but Father Solomon is killed near the end of the film. Valerie is quite direct about her desire for Peter, even though they are prevented from consummating the relationship. Valerie defeats the wolf herself and leaves the village to wait for Peter, even though he has become a werewolf.

2. **Describe how the film shows Valerie's transition from childhood to full adulthood.**

   Valerie learns the truth about her mother's affair and her dead sister's paternity, and begins to withdraw from her mother. After Valerie encounters the wolf, she is jailed and separated from the rest of the village. When she escapes, she stabs Peter, thinking he is the wolf. At her grandmother's house, she learns that her father is the wolf, and that she could become a werewolf. She refuses her father's offer and kills her father. She realizes the truth about her father and that Peter was true to her all along. She sees her family and the world in a different way now that all the lies have been exposed. Although the village is now safe from the wolf, the village still lives in fear. Valerie no longer wants to live there, finding more freedom in the forest, and finding there is less to be feared living alone. At the end of the film, Valerie waits for Peter, smiling as he returns to her in his wolf form. She has conquered her fears and accepted the complexities of adult life.

3. **Explain how the film portrays the ideas of a child's dissatisfaction with parents.**

   Valerie resents her mother for arranging her marriage to the wealthy Henry and discouraging Valerie's relationship with her true love Peter. When Valerie learns that her older sister was in love with Henry, she is angry at her mother. When Valerie learns the real reason for her mother's actions was due to her mother's affair with Henry's father, she is angrier still. Valerie loves her father, but this changes when Valerie learns that her father is the wolf. By the end of the film, Valerie has fulfilled the child's desire to get rid of both of her parents. She kills her father the wolf, and moves to the forest, away from her mother.

20.   *Seinfeld,* "The Soup"

Film Data

Year: 1994, Season 6, episode 7

Director: Andy Ackerman

Length: 23 minutes

Rated: TV/PG

Characters/Actors

Jerry Seinfeld: Jerry Seinfeld

Elaine Benes: Julia Louis-Dreyfus

Kramer: Michael Richards

George: Jason Alexander

Kenny Bania: Steve Hytner

Connection to Chapters

Chapter 30. Applying Theory: Meals in the Bible (Mary Douglas)

Recommended Scenes

The scene of Kenny offering Jerry the suit occurs at 00:02:26 through 00:03:13.

The scene of Kenny making the deal for the meal occurs at 00:04:45 through 00:05:38.

The scene of Jerry and Kenny having soup and a meal occurs at 00:11:05 through 00:12:08.

The scene of Jerry and Elaine discussing the issue of soup as a meal occurs at 00:12:12 through 00:13:12.

The scene of Jerry, George, and Kenny in the coffeeshop occurs at 00:14:08 through 00:15:33.

Instructor Viewing Information

Students should be familiar with the *Seinfeld* series, but even if they are not, little explanation will be necessary. The episode stands alone and students should enjoy the characters and humor. The episode focuses directly on the many meanings of meals and should be an excellent and dynamic way to discuss the concepts of food as code, the social boundaries determined by meals, and the meal as a ritual.

Synopsis

Kenny Bania (Hytner), an annoying acquaintance of Jerry's (Seinfeld), tells Jerry that he has worked out so much that his brand new designer suit doesn't fit him. Kenny offers to give Jerry the suit and Jerry reluctantly agrees. When Kenny drops off the suit to Jerry, Kramer (Richards) comments on Kenny's generosity. Kenny says he does not want anything for the suit, but perhaps Jerry would buy him a meal sometime. Jerry does not want to spend any time with Kenny, but Kenny insists on dinner that evening at a nice restaurant. At the restaurant, Kenny orders soup, saying he is not very hungry and he will save the meal for another time. Jerry wants to count their dinner as the meal, but Kenny insists that soup is not a meal. Later in the episode, Jerry and his friend Elaine (Louis-Dreyfus) discuss the meal. When Kenny runs into Jerry and George at a coffeeshop, he insists on joining them. Kenny asks the waitresses about soup, and Jerry suggests that Kenny order a sandwich. Kenny orders soup and a sandwich. Jerry says this counts as the meal owed, but Kenny disagrees. Disgusted by the whole incident, Jerry gives the designer suit to Elaine's boyfriend.

Discussion Questions

1. **Explain how the episode portrays the idea of food as a code.**

   Most of the episode centers on the disagreement between Jerry and Kenny as to what constitutes a meal. Jerry believes the act of sitting in a restaurant at dinnertime constitutes a meal. Jerry is willing to pay for anything Kenny might order, but Kenny chooses soup. Kenny makes it clear that for him, the one simple dish of soup is not a meal. In fact, he specifically states that he will have soup and save the meal for another time. Later on in the episode, Elaine tells Jerry that the size and type of soup can determine if soup is deemed a meal. She states that consommé is not a meal, but a hearty soup like chicken noodle or gumbo may be a meal. Elaine also states that crumbling crackers into a soup could make it a meal. She ends the conversation by asking Jerry if Kenny had the soup in a bowl or cup, implying the amount of soup consumed may determine if the soup was in fact a meal. Near the end of the episode, Kenny has a sandwich and soup in the coffee shop. Jerry firmly states that this is a meal, but Kenny still disagrees. His idea of a meal is dinner in a restaurant.

2. **Describe how the episode shows the social boundaries determined by the food meanings.**

Kenny wants to think of Jerry as his friend and wants to spend time with Jerry. Jerry is annoyed by Kenny and wants to avoid spending time with him. Kenny maneuvers Jerry into agreeing to buy him a meal, which Kenny specifies as dinner. Kenny arranges dinner in a nice restaurant and intentionally orders soup, which he clearly believes is not a meal. He does this to spend time with Jerry and to force Jerry to spend additional time with him in order to fulfill Jerry's promise to buy Kenny a meal. When Jerry and Kenny run into each other at the coffeeshop, Jerry wants to buy Kenny soup and a sandwich and count it as a meal. Kenny makes it clear that his idea of a meal is a more substantial dinner at a nice restaurant. Kenny states that using the lunch at a coffeeshop to count as a meal is not a proper thank-you for the gift of the suit.

3. **Describe how the episode portrays meals as the line between intimacy and distance.**

Despite the gift of the expensive suit, Jerry still does not want to share a meal with Kenny. After he reluctantly agrees to the meal, he states that he would rather make his own suit than share a meal with Kenny. Jerry does not consider Kenny a close friend and does not want to have a meal with him. During this episode, Jerry, George, and Elaine share several meals together. They are close friends, and the waitress at the coffeeshop knows them because they all eat together so often. When Jerry and George see Kenny coming into the coffeeshop, Jerry and George both slide to edge of the booth, so Kenny will not be able to join them. Kenny does not recognize this and asks them to slide over. Jerry does not consider Kenny to be a friend who is intimate enough to share lunch with him at a coffeeshop. But Kenny does not consider lunch at a coffeeshop intimate enough, and wants to have an even more intimate dinner with Jerry.

21. Serenity

Film Data

Year: 2005

Director: Joss Whedon

Length: 119 minutes

Rated: PG-13

Characters/Actors

Nathan Fillion:	Mal
Gina Torres:	Zoë
Alan Tudyk:	Wash
Morena Baccarin:	Inara
Adam Baldwin:	Jayne
Jewel Staite:	Kaylee
Sean Maher:	Simon
Summer Glau:	River
Ron Glass:	Shepherd Derrial Book
Chiwetel Ejiofor:	The Operative

Connection to Chapters

Chapter 41. *Stagecoach* and *Firefly:* The Journey into the Unknown in Westerns and Science Fiction

Recommended Scenes

The scene of River's teacher explaining the history of the Alliance occurs at the start of the film through 00:02:13.

The scene of the Operator asking Mal to settle things like civilized men occurs at 00:53:40.

The scene of Shepherd's death and the Operator justifying his actions occurs at 01:05:40 through 01:09:09.

The scene of Mal threatening to shoot his crew if they do not help him occurs at 01:10:17.

The scene of the crew watching the video explanation of the experiment on Miranda occurs at 01:18:04 through 01:20:01.

The scene of Mal telling his crew that someone needs to speak for the people harmed occurs at 01:20:45 through 01:22:38.

The scene of River defeating the Reavers, Mal battling the Operator, and the resolution of the story occurs at 01:41:49 through the end of the film.

Instructor Viewing Information

Serenity continues the story of the cult television series *Firefly*. The film also provides background and explanations for some of the plot points raised in the series. Those not familiar with the series or the film should be able to understand the plot with a minimum of explanation. Students should enjoy the characters, futuristic setting, and exciting action sequences. *Serenity* should provide an excellent way to discuss the role of science fiction in mythology and to examine the way the film reflects the concerns of its audience.

Synopsis

Serenity takes place 500 years in the future in a solar system governed by an interplanetary body called the Alliance. Captain Mal (Fillion) and his crew—Zoë (Torres), Wash (Tudyk), Jayne (Baldwin), and Kaylee (Staite)—eke out a living on their cargo ship *Serenity*. They also hide a brother and sister, Simon (Maher) and River (Glau), from the Alliance. River was part of an Alliance experiment and is now unstable. The Alliance has been chasing River ever since Simon freed her. The situation has become more serious, and Mal elects to let the sibling stay. The Alliance is using a deadly and persistent agent known as The Operative (Ejiofor) to capture and kill River. While running from the Alliance, the Serenity crew must also contend with the vicious Reavers. The crew finally learns that the Alliance performed an experiment on the planet Miranda that made the population too docile to live. However, a small part of that population became vicious killers called the Reavers. River knows this secret and is a threat to the Alliance. Mal and his crew find video evidence of this and risk their lives to broadcast this message. Wash is killed, Simon and Kaylee are wounded, and River kills the attacking Reavers. Mal wounds the Operator and broadcasts the tape. When the Operator learns the truth about the Alliance, he prevents its soldiers from killing Mal and his crew. The film ends with Mal and his crew continuing on, with River as copilot. They have damaged the Alliance and are safe for now.

Discussion Questions

1. **Explain how the film explores the idea of individualism and the group.**

It is very clear that Mal believes he has sole authority on the ship, and those that choose to stay with the ship must submit to his decisions. The crew does not vote on decisions. When the crew balks at Mal's plan to fly into Reaver territory, Mal explains that they can leave. He states that if they choose to stay, he will shoot them if they do not help. But they do listen. The crew shares Mal's feelings about the Alliance oppressing the individual. Mal also expresses the idea that a "man has to stand on his own." Mal often acts as if he only cares about himself and then his crew. This contrasts with the ideas expressed by the Operator, who believes he is justified in acting like a monster to serve a greater good. The Operator does not question the orders of the Alliance, because he believes he is creating a "world without sin." Of course, in the end the Operator sees the truth about the Alliance. But Mal also shows he cares quite a lot about others. He explains that the Alliance believes that they can "make people better" and will try to do so again. This is similar to what River tells her teacher in the beginning of the film, saying that people oppose the Alliance because they do not like to be told what to think. This very much goes against Mal's philosophy of the individual's free will. Mal and his crew risk their lives to reveal the truth about the Alliance and to protect others from more harm. Mal asks his crew to join him in this battle, saying that someone must speak for the people harmed. In the end, the crew risks their lives to save the galaxy. Mal shows that he really believes the individual is not selfish, but selfless.

2. **Explain the film's underlying assumptions about civilization.**

The film begins with a flashback of River as a child being taught the history of the Alliance. The teacher explains that the Alliance was a "beacon of civilization" and those who fought against the Alliance were savages. The teacher explains that now that the Alliance won the war, everyone can enjoy the benefits of true civilization. When Mal encounters the Operator, he tells Mal that he hopes they can settle their differences like civilized men. Of course, the Operator is an assassin who kills children. The Alliance created the Reavers and kills those who fight against it. In the film, those that represent "civilization" are barbaric and evil.

3. **Describe the film's underlying assumptions about civilization and alternate communities.**

The characters in the film create their own community as an alternative to traditional civilization. The crew has some of the characteristics of a family, but operates more as a community. Wash and Zoë are married, and Zoë and Mal fought together in the war and have a close relationship, but other relationships are not as clear. The group confines its loyalty to the crew of the ship, and who is crew and who is not becomes an important distinction. When Mal argues with Simon about River, Mal explains that Simon and River are guests, not crew. Simon counters by arguing that by performing medical services, he has earned his keep. Mal retorts that he needs to look out for "me and mine." He explains that only includes those he deems part of the crew. When River and Simon leave the ship after an argument with Mal, Kaylee complains. When Zoë points out that it Mal didn't cause River and Simon to be fugitives, Kaylee replies that Mal could have chosen to "make them family." But through the course of the film, Mal and the others choose to expand this definition of crew and community. He relents and chooses to protect River and Simon, and the others agree. When Mal and the others find that former crew member Shepherd Derrial Book (Glass) has been wounded, Mal comforts the dying man. When Shepherd says that he will not be around and he is not one of Mal's crew, Mal answers, "Yes you are." Throughout the film, Mal and the others expand the definition of crew and family to include emotional attachments. After the battle is over, Mal offers to take prostitute and former crew member Inara (Baccarin) back to her planet. When he asks if she is ready to return to civilized life, she indicates she would prefer to stay with Mal in their alternate civilization. At the end of the film, Mal allows River to be his copilot. As he explains how to fly the ship, he informs her that love is what keeps the ship in the air and what makes the ship home.

4. **Describe the film's underlying assumptions about the government and science.**

In the world of *Serenity,* scientific advancements have made space travel possible. Terra forming is used to make planets habitable by humans, since the earth is no longer viable. But science and the government are viewed as entities not to be trusted. The Alliance is seen as a corrupt and controlling government body, one the crew avoids. The crew knows that the Alliance used River in harmful experiments. When Mal first encounters the Operator, the Operator explains that the Alliance is not an "evil empire." But Mal learns the Alliance is evil when the crew discovers the secret of the planet Miranda. The planet was made habitable for humans, but chemicals were put in the air processors to make the population calmer. This caused the population to lose the will to live and made a small percentage of them vicious killers called the Reavers. Any good done by the terra farming is far outweighed by the evil done. Mal and his crew see the government as an entity that uses science to control people.

22. Sita Sings the Blues

Film Data

Year: 2008

Director: Nina Paley

Length: 82 minutes

Rated: N/A

Characters/Actors

Annette Hanshaw: Sita (singing) (archive sound)

Aseem Chhabra: Narrator, Shadow Puppet 1 (voice)

Bhavana Nagulapally: Narrator, Shadow Puppet 2 (voice)

Manish Acharya: Narrator, Shadow Puppet 3 (voice)

Reena Shah: Sita (voice)

Sanjiv Jhaveri: Dave/Dasharatha/Ravana/Dhobi/Valmiki (voice)

Debargo Sanyal: Rama (voice)

Nina Paley: Nina (voice)

Connection to Chapters

Chapter 18. India: The *Ramayana*

Recommended Scenes

The scene of Ravana kidnapping Sita occurs at 00:17:01 through 00:22:00.

The scene of Sita refusing to give in to Ravana and the narrators commenting on Sita's actions occurs at 00:27:33 through 00:31:34.

The scene of Sita's kidnapping and Ravana's proposal occurs at 00:17:17 through 00:24:01.

The scene of Sita's rescue, Rama's rejection, and the test of the funeral pyre occurs at 00:37:21 through 00:42:51.

The scene of Sita and Rama forgiving each other occurs at 00:43:27.

The scene of the Indian dance occurs at 00:51:05 through 00:54:26

The scene of Sita's sons learning songs of praise for Rama occurs at 01:04:43 through 01:06:25.

The final scene of Sita being taken into the womb of mother earth begins at 01:10:59.

Instructor Viewing Information

Although the credits for this animated musical say that it is based on the *Ramayana* by Valmiki, *Sita Sings the Blues* includes some Western elements. The film is in English and uses songs by 1920s jazz vocalist Annette Hanshaw to emphasize Sita's emotions throughout the story. Interspersed with the story of Sita (Shah) and Rama (Sanyal) is a modern tale of Dave (Jhaveri) and Nina (Paley), who live in San Francisco with their cat, but eventually break up. The film also uses three narrators (Chhabra, Nagulapally, and Acharya) with Indian accents who tell the story of Sita by piecing together what they remember of the story, commenting on the story, and offering their opinions. Students will enjoy the humor and contemporary opinions expressed by the three narrators. Students should also appreciate the parallels between the relationships of Nina and Dave and Sita and Rama, as well as how the film focuses on the way that the turmoil in each relationship affects the female characters. This charming and vibrant film is an excellent way to begin a discussion of the *Ramayana,* the concept of *dharma,* and the resonance of this myth in present times.

Synopsis

The film focuses on the part of the *Ramayana* that relates to Sita's kidnapping and rescue by Rama. Rama agrees to be banished for fourteen years to the forest, and his wife Sita insists on accompanying him. Ravana (Jhaveri) is persuaded to use trickery to kidnap Sita. He proposes marriage to Sita and threatens her with death if she refuses. He gives her two months to decide, but Sita remains true to Rama. Rama rescues Sita, but then he rejects her, saying she must have been defiled during the time she was kidnapped. Sita asks for the funeral pyre to prove her purity. She is rescued by the gods, and Rama and Sita reunite. However, later Rama says that his subjects do not respect him because of Sita, and he banishes Sita. A pregnant Sita goes to the forest and gives birth to twin boys. Rama finds them many years later and welcomes his sons back to the kingdom. However, Rama asks Sita to prove her purity again. Sita agrees and says that if she is completely pure, mother earth should take her back into her womb. The film ends when Sita is taken back into the womb of mother earth. Sita sings and Rama sheds a tear.

Discussion Questions

1. **Describe how the characters in the film illustrate the concept of *dharma*.**

   The king believes Rama is the ideal man, but he must banish Rama to keep a promise to his wife, even though he describes her as "evil." The narrators explain that Indian men must keep promises to their wives. The film shows that Rama does not argue with the king, and the narrators comment on this. Even though Rama does not want Sita to accompany him because he does not want to endanger her, Sita insists that she go with Rama. She says that a woman's place is next to her husband. Sita even sings a song about her devotion. When Sita is captured by Ravana, she refuses to marry him and insists she must wait for her husband, as that is her obligation. Sita remains pure. The narrators wonder why Sita did not escape when she had the chance. They opine that Sita feels she needs to wait for Rama to rescue her in order to give him the glory. Sita does not get angry with her husband when he questions her purity, but instead asks for the funeral pyre to prove her worthiness. She says that she cannot bear to live if her husband doubts her. When Sita is proven pure, she tells Rama that she forgives him, as she lives only for him. Later in the film, Rama banishes Sita because he feels his subjects do not respect him. Rama puts his kingdom and his ability to rule ahead of his love for Sita. When Sita is banished and raises her two sons in the forest, she allows Valmiki (Jhaveri) to teach her boys to sing praises of Rama. Their song emphasizes the fact the Rama does what he should do as a ruler, despite the fact that he banished Sita. The songs states that Rama is a good ruler because he put his duty first.

2. **Explain how the film shows how the Hindu gods take a personal interest in the lives of humans.**

   Although Rama appears to be part god, he has human problems and emotions. The film does not show that he has the powers of a god, but only the rights and obligations of a ruler. When Sita asks for the funeral pyre as Rama doubts her purity, the gods intervene. The film shows Sita singing about a man being mean to her as she undergoes the trial by fire. A singed Sita continues to sing as a large and powerful figure carries an unharmed Sita out of the fire. The narrators explain that the gods sent a flying chariot to return Sita and Rama to their kingdom. Near the end of the film, Rama again asks Sita to prove her purity. When Sita asks mother earth to take her back to her womb if Sita is pure, the gods oblige. The film ends with a goddess arising and taking an eager Sita into her womb. Sita sings a happy song in the womb of mother earth, as she disappears into the ground.

3. **Describe how the film incorporates Indian traditions surrounding the myth.**

The film's three narrators seem to know different aspects of the story, and often show confusion about the details. They often are unclear or disagree about the sequence of events, as they try to recall the stories they learned. The film incorporates the idea that this myth was spoken and passed on before it was written down. The film refers to the written version by Valmiki, by making Valmiki a character in the film. In the film, Valmiki teaches Sita's sons songs of praise for Rama, and also writes down Sita's story. The film uses brighter and more theatrical animation for Sita and Rama during the musical numbers. This emphasizes the grandeur of the story. The film also accomplishes this with a musical number devoted to an Indian dance performance of the story.

23. Stagecoach

Film Data

Year: 1939

Director: John Ford

Length: 96 minutes

Rated: N/A

Characters/Actors

Claire Trevor:	Dallas
John Wayne:	Ringo Kid
Andy Devine:	Buck
John Carradine:	Hatfield
Thomas Mitchell:	Doc Boone
Louise Platt:	Lucy Mallory
George Bancroft:	Curley
Donald Meek:	Peacock
Berton Churchill:	Gatewood

Connection to Chapters

Chapter 41. *Stagecoach* and *Firefly:* Journey into the Unknown in Westerns and Science Fiction

Recommended Scenes

The scene of the Law and Order League occurs at 00:06:49.

The scene of the group voting to keep going occurs at 00:25:58.

The scene of the group cooing over Lucy's baby occurs at 00:48:34 through 00:49:56.

The scene of Doc Boone toasting the group occurs at 01:10:20.

The scene of the battle with the Apaches and the ensuing rescue by the army occurs at 01:10:23 through 01:17:10.

The scene of Curley and the doctor letting Ringo and Dallas get away occurs at 01:33:49 through the end of the film.

Instructor Viewing Information

The acclaimed *Stagecoach* is a black-and-white Western directed by John Ford. While some students may find the pace a bit slow by contemporary standards, many will enjoy the complex characters and the fine filmmaking. While the fight sequences look much different than those in more contemporary films, the action sequences remain raw and exciting. *Stagecoach* provides excellent examples of the travelers as family, community, morality, and the journey fraught with peril. The timeless themes present in this excellent film should provide the framework for a lively discussion of this Western's influence on science fiction.

Synopsis

Stagecoach chronicles the journey of six passengers and their drivers from the town of Tonto to Lordsburg. The stagecoach is driven by Buck (Devine) and lawman Curley (Bancroft), who goes along to look for fugitive Ringo (Wayne). The passengers include prostitute Dallas (Trevor) and drunken Doc Boone (Mitchell). Both have been thrown out of town by the Law and Order League. Corrupt banker Gatewood (Churchill), whiskey salesman Peacock (Meek), gambler Hatfield (Carradine), and pregnant Lucy (Platt), who travels to meet her husband, make up the rest of the passenger list. The group soon picks up escaped prisoner Ringo. Curley intends to arrest Ringo, but Ringo's skills are needed on the journey. Along the way, the passengers get to know and care about each other, all help Lucy deliver her baby, and Ringo and Dallas fall in love. The group fights off attacking Apaches and Hatfield is killed. The rest of the group arrives safely in Lordsburg. Ringo settles a score with two brothers who wronged him and agrees to return to jail. Dallas says she will marry Ringo. As the film ends, it appears Curley will allow Ringo to escape to his ranch for a life with Dallas.

1. **Explain how the film questions conventional ideas of morality.**

    Near the beginning of the film, Doc Boone and Dallas are thrown out of town by the unpleasant women in the Law and Order League. The women in the town are judgmental and superficial. The women surrounding Lucy are shocked that she is willing to travel with a prostitute. They also view Doc Boone's medical abilities with contempt. Lucy also refuses to sit near Dallas while eating or in the stagecoach, and rebuffs several kind overtures by Dallas. Likewise, Hatfield ignores Dallas, and is very solicitous of Lucy, referring to her as a "lady." Ringo reminds Hatfield that there is another lady in their company. Hatfield also sneers that Doc Boone is not much of a credit to the medical profession. When Hatfield also objects to the doctor smoking in front of a lady, Doc Boone points out that he treated a man who had been shot by a gentleman like Hatfield. Doc Boone refers to the hypocrisy of judging by appearances. Hatfield seems very class-conscious, but he is a gambler, and perhaps a thief. Of course, Doc Boone is capable enough to deliver Lucy's baby with Dallas' help. By the end of the film, Lucy changes her mind about Dallas and expresses her gratitude. Ringo, who is an escaped convict, also shows his honorable side when he agrees to allow Curley to return him to jail. He also gives Curley his word that he will not try to escape. Peacock, the whiskey salesman, treats all with kindness. When the passengers start to argue, he implores them to treat each other with a little "Christian charity." The characters with the questionable professions of whiskey salesman, prostitute, and criminal are the passengers who show integrity, bravery, and compassion. The characters who appear to be decent moral people by conventional standards are shown to be small-minded and mean.

2. **Describe the film's underlying assumptions about civilization and alternate communities.**

    The stagecoach passengers travel from the supposedly civilized town of Tonto to the town of Lordsburg. Both communities have citizens who feel they are morally superior to others. The stagecoach is small and people must sit close to one another. There is a comedic effect each time another person joins the group. But in a sense, this is the beginning of this stagecoach community. By the time the group arrives at Lordsburg, Lucy has changed her mind about Dallas. She wants to help Dallas, but as they say goodbye, Lucy and Dallas appear to know that they cannot be friends in this town. In between the two towns lies land that one might consider uncivilized. Here, the group forms their own community and makes rules that accommodate all of their needs. When the group must decide if they should continue on without the army, Curley asks for a vote. As a group, they decide to carry on. When Lucy is ready to have her baby, everyone but the banker is concerned and wants to help. When they baby is born, Dallas holds the infant, and the men stand around the baby and coo. The baby is welcomed into this community by its members. When Ringo asks Dallas to run away with him, she says she cannot leave Lucy and her baby. The bonds of this community begin to resemble the bonds of a family. This alternate community becomes a place of compassion. As the group journeys on, Doc Boone proposes they toast as they may never again meet socially. He assumes that should they survive this journey, they will go back to their own lives and communities. Despite what they have shared on the stagecoach, this community is temporary, and may not endure. But it does endure in spirit, as each person is changed by it. Hatfield is killed while helping the others. Dallas and Ringo stay together. At the very end of the film, Doc Boone and Curley allow Ringo and Dallas to run away together. Doc Boone, who disparages civilization at the start of the film, does so at the end. He is glad Dallas and Ringo got away. Curley, the lawman, agrees. He has changed his idea of justice in a civilized society to a broader idea of justice in this alternate community. He laughs and offers to buy the doctor a drink. These unlikely friends end the film laughing, agreeing, and helping Dallas and Ringo. In a sense, this alternate community lives on.

3. **Describe the film's underlying assumptions about the military.**

In *Stagecoach,* the military is viewed with respect. However, the characters know that there are times when they must rely only on themselves. At the start of the film, the group is warned by soldiers that their journey will take them through treacherous territory. The military can only accompany them so far. A soldier explains to Curley that the army has no authority over him, and will not stop him. The soldier explains that he cannot continue on because he must obey his orders. When the belligerent banker threatens to file a complaint against the military for abandoning the group, the soldier treats the banker with courtesy. "That is your privilege sir," he answers. After the army leaves the group, the banker angrily states that the army has no right to leave its citizens undefended. Ringo defends the military, stating that the army "has its hands full." Near the end of the film, the group is outnumbered and losing the battle to the Apaches. But they are rescued by the army and their lives are saved.

24. Star Trek II: The Wrath of Khan

Film Data

Year: 1982

Director: Nicholas Meyer

Length: 113 minutes

Rated: PG

Characters/Actors

William Shatner: Admiral James T. Kirk

Leonard Nimoy: Captain Spock

DeForest Kelley: Dr. McCoy

Kirstie Alley: Lt. Saavik

Ricardo Montalban: Khan

Bibi Besch: Dr. Carol Marcus

Merritt Butrick: Dr. David Marcus

Walter Koenig: Mr. Chekov

Connection to Chapters

Chapter 41. *Stagecoach* and *Firefly:* Journeys into the Unknown in Westerns and Science Fiction

Recommended Scenes

The scene of Chekov discussing the genetic engineering experiment occurs at 00:18:11.

The scene of Spock talking to Kirk about the needs of the many and Kirk's destiny occurs at 00:39:22 through 00:40:11.

The scene of Dr. Marcus explaining Project Genesis and the ensuing debate about it occurs at 00:43:20 through 00:46:04.

The scene of the start of the battle between Khan and Kirk begins at 00:51:07.

The scene of Khan trying to detonate Project Genesis occurs at 01:30:12.

The scene of Spock sacrificing himself and his farewell to Kirk occurs at 01:31:48 through 01:39:12.

The scene of Spock's funeral and the resolution of the story occurs at 01:39:41 through the end of the film.

Instructor Viewing Information

The original *Star Trek* series ran from 1966 through 1969. The series spawned other television series, as well as eleven films between 1979 through 2009. *Star Trek II: The Wrath of Khan* features the cast and characters from the original series, as well Khan (Montalban), a villain from a past series episode. Even students who are not fans of *Star Trek* should have some familiarity with the characters and actors. While the film may seem dated in parts, students should enjoy the action and humor in this fine film. *Star Trek II: The Wrath of Khan* is an excellent way to begin a discussion of science fiction and myth. The film also provides rich examples of the changing values of the group, the individual, and science, and should lead to a vibrant discussion.

Synopsis

The film begins with a training simulation involving members of the former crew of the starship *Enterprise* and new recruits. But problems force Admiral Kirk (Shatner) to take control of the ship and investigate, using both his old crew and the recruits. Another starship has encountered Kirk's old enemy Khan. Khan is ruthless in his attempt to steal Project Genesis, a life-generating technology developed by Kirk's old flame Dr. Marcus (Besch) and her son David (Butrick), who is later revealed to be Kirk's son. Khan also wants to get revenge on Kirk. A battle ensues. The battle with Khan allows old friends Kirk, Spock (Nimoy), and McCoy (Kelley) to explore their feelings about their life choices, growing older, and their enduring friendships. Both McCoy and Spock believe that Kirk should return to being a captain. As the space battle continues, Kirk manages to outmaneuver Khan and defeat him. But Khan has obtained Project Genesis and uses it as a weapon to try to destroy the *Enterprise*. The *Enterprise* suffers losses, and it appears Project Genesis will detonate and destroy the ship. Spock prevents this by sacrificing his life. After Spock's funeral, Kirk and the crew send Spock's remains to a planet being regenerated by

Project Genesis. At the end of the film, Kirk states that he hopes to return to that planet soon. Kirk says that he feels young again, and sees life's many possibilities.

Discussion Questions

1. Explain how the film reflects the audience's attitudes about science.

We learn that Khan was part of a late-twentieth-century experiment involving genetic engineering. Mr. Chekov (Koenig) expresses some disdain when explaining this. Apparently, Khan was part of a superior race of humans. The film reflects the discomfort the audience has with the idea of genetic engineering. It appears that in the twenty-third century, where the film occurs, people are also uncomfortable with the idea of genetic engineering. No one in the film ever alludes to potential benefits of this kind of science. However, Project Genesis is viewed differently. Dr. Marcus and her son are portrayed as idealists, who see the potential for good in their life-generating research. Although Dr. McCoy expresses some reservations about Project Genesis, Kirk and the others embrace the possibilities for this research. They point out that this research could help with food and overpopulation. This is consistent with a science fiction series about space travel made possible by scientific advances. But the film acknowledges reservations that the audience may have about the misuse of science. Although Project Genesis was intended to be used for good, Khan tries to use it to kill Kirk and the others, and wants it for his own nefarious purposes. When McCoy and Spock discuss the moral implications of this research, Spock points out that history shows that it is always easier to destroy than to create. Science is embraced, but its potential abuses are not ignored.

2. Describe the film's underlying assumptions about religion.

At the beginning of the film, Lt. Saavik (Alley) asks Kirk for suggestions after the she fails in the simulation. He responds by saying "prayer." Religion exists in some way, but it does not appear to be very important in the lives of the characters. The film assumes that religion is important to few people. Dr. McCoy represents this group. However, the concept of religion is vague and undefined. McCoy is the only one to voice objections to Project Genesis. He mentions biblical creation, but does so by saying that "according to myth, the world was created in six says." He wonders if humans are capable of using such technology. McCoy also says that he is afraid that this technology could create "universal Armageddon." Religious thought is present, but it seems to stay in the background.

3. **Explain how the film portrays the values of the group over the values of the individual.**

In the world created in the film, the military is a group viewed with respect. Starfleet is comprised of humans and other peaceful species. The chain of command is clear, but equality exists. The captain Kirk is training is both female and a Vulcan. It is assumed that those in the military act with morality and for the good of all. When a problem arises near the simulation, Starfleet command orders Kirk and the *Enterprise* to investigate, even though the ship was being used for training and filled with young recruits. Spock insists that Kirk assume command of the ship, as he is the senior office on board, and Spock is only in charge when the ship is being used for training. When Kirk demurs and says that Spock should take command, Spock explains that he has no ego to bruise. He explains that logic dictates that the needs of the many outweigh the needs of the few. It is best for all that Kirk take command. This philosophy is repeated at the end of the film. Spock sacrifices his life to save the ship. He tells Kirk not to grieve for him, as the needs of the many outweigh the needs of the few, or the one. But the film also shows that the characters value individual fulfillment. Both McCoy and Spock tell Kirk that he made a mistake when he stopped being a captain. Spock explains that being a captain was Kirk's "first best destiny." At times, fulfilling your desires may also be what is best for the group.

4. **Describe the film's underlying assumptions about the place of human beings in the cosmos.**

Star Trek II: The Wrath of Khan imagines a world where races, genders, and species coexist peacefully. But aside from Spock and Saavik, all of the characters are human. Humans have advanced enough to command ships and use technology to travel through the galaxy. At Spock's funeral, a tearful Kirk says that of all the souls he encountered in his space travels, his friend Spock's was "the most human." Kirk feels this to be the highest compliment he could pay his friend. This is a bit undercut by the fact that Spock would have likely objected to this characterization, as Spock saw himself as a Vulcan. Spock believed his self-sacrifice was the result of logic, not emotion. At the very end of the film, Spock speaks the words from every episode of the television show in a voiceover. "Space, the final frontier. . . . These are the continuing voyages of the Starship *Enterprise*. Its ongoing mission is to explore strange new worlds, to seek out new life forms and new civilizations, to boldly go where no man has gone before." This states the philosophy of both the television series and the film. Humans are meant to continue to explore the cosmos and the unknown.

25. Star Wars Episode Four: A New Hope

Film Data

Year: 1977

Director: George Lucas

Length: 121 minutes

Rated: PG

Characters/Actors

Mark Hamill:	Luke Skywalker
Harrison Ford:	Han Solo
Carrie Fisher:	Princess Leia Organa
Anthony Daniels:	C-3P0
Alec Guinness:	Ben Obi-Wan Kenobi
Kenny Baker	R2-D2
David Prowse	Darth Vader
James Earl Jones	Darth Vader (voice)

Connection to Chapters

Chapter 15. Theory: Joseph Campbell, *The Hero with a Thousand Faces* (Dave Whomsley)

Recommended Scenes

The scene of Luke's initial conversation with the androids and the message from Princess Leia occurs at 00:20:51 through 00:22:57.

The scene of the first conversation between Ben and Luke occurs at 00:31:09 through 00:36:32.

The scene in the Mos Eisley bar occurs at 00:43:35.

The scene of Luke receiving Jedi training from Ben occurs at 00:58:20.

The scene of Luke, Han, and Leia trapped in the "belly of the whale" occurs at 01:17:01.

The scene of the light saber battle between Ben and Darth Vader occurs at 01:27:35.

The scene of Han refusing to join Luke and Luke discussing it with Leia occurs at 01:39:00 through 01:40:22.

The scene of the last part of the battle and the resolution occurs at 01:51:00 through the end of the film.

Instructor Viewing Information

The 1977 *Star Wars* was the first film in a series of six. To date, the last film was released in 2005. The most recent three films were prequels. *Episode IV: A New Hope* was later added to the title of the 1977 *Star Wars*. Students will probably be familiar with the series, although they may not have been exposed to the first film. Students will enjoy the action sequences and the by-now-familiar terms and characters. *Star Wars* is an excellent way to discuss Joseph Campbell's ideas, especially because of the direct influence of Campbell on George Lucas' work. This film will provide a good way to illustrate the hero cycle described by Campbell.

Synopsis

The film takes place at unspecified time in the future when space travel is common. The film opens with a written introduction on the screen explaining that there is a civil war against the ruling galactic empire. Working with the empire, Darth Vader (Prowse/Jones) kidnaps Princess Leia (Fisher) in an attempt to steal plans for a lethal weapon. Aspiring pilot Luke Skywalker (Hamill) has the job of taking care of two androids, R2-D2 (Baker) and C-3P0 (Daniels). While working on them, he finds an old video message from Princess Leia asking for help from Ben Obi-Wan Kenobi (Guinness). When Luke finds Ben Kenobi, he learns about his father, a Jedi knight, and is given his father's weapon, the light saber. Luke joins Ben on the mission to help rescue Princess Leia. Ben trains Luke and they recruit a mercenary pilot, Han Solo (Ford), to help them. Together they rescue Princess Leia and battle the empire. Ben lets Darth Vader kill him, knowing that Luke will continue the fight. During the final battle, Han Solo helps Luke Skywalker defeat the empire forces. The film ends with Princess Leia giving Luke and Han medals.

Discussion Questions

1. **Describe how Luke Skywalker follows the steps in the hero's journey as outlined by Joseph Campbell.**

When Luke hears Princess Leia' message asking Obi-Wan Kenobi for help, he immediately sets out to find Ben Kenobi, despite his uncle's objections. When Ben asks Luke to help him, Luke first refuses the call to adventure. But after Luke's uncle and aunt are killed, Luke accepts the adventure and eagerly embraces learning the ways of the force. As Luke and Ben prepare to rescue Princess Leia, the older Ben acts as a protective figure for Luke. He provides Luke with a supernatural weapon, the light saber, and teaches him how to use it. Ben also instructs Luke on the ways of the force. In the Mos Eisley bar, Ben fights an attacker who threatens to harm Luke. After Ben's death, Luke hears Ben's voice giving him important advice about how to use the force to win a battle. The events that take place in Mos Eisley bar provide good example of the hero on the edge of an adventure. In the bar, Luke Skywalker meets several unusual characters, characters that have already been there and can tell tales about the places the hero intends to go. Later in the film, Luke, Leia, and Han are trapped in a trash compacter. This is an example of the belly of the whale step. Luke is pulled into a slimy pool of water, and a strange looking creature attempts to kill him. It is unclear if Luke is actually swallowed by the creature, but he does disappear with the creature beneath the slimy water. By the end of the film, Luke is able to use what Ben taught him about the force to defeat the agents of the empire who are pursuing him. He even turns off his ship's computer and trusts the force. In this film the adventure ends when Luke receives a medal from Princess Leia. Luke has achieved illumination and understanding. Before his adventure, he was somewhat childlike. But now he knows of his heritage, realizes his skill and bravery, and understands how to use the force.

2. **Describe how Han Solo follows the steps in the hero's journey as outlined by Joseph Campbell.**

Han Solo insists that he is only interested in money. He agrees to help Luke and Ben for a fee. He is reluctant to help rescue Leia and only agrees to help when Luke promises him riches. He initially answers the call to adventure for monetary reasons, but continues helping Luke. Like Luke, Han also experiences the belly of the whale in the trash compacter. Even after they survive this, Han tells Leia, "I am in it for the money. I do not care about you or your revolution." After they escape the trash compacter and rescue the princess, Luke asks Han to stay and help fight the empire. Han declines. Although he scoffs at the idea of the force, he says farewell to Luke by saying, "May the force be with you." Perhaps this is the beginning of Han's spiritual enlightenment. Later, Han returns to help Luke in battle, despite his earlier refusal. After the battle is won, Han laughingly tells Luke that he can take the credit and the money. Leia tells Han that she knew there was more to him than money. Han has also achieved illumination and understanding. Han understands something more about himself. Like Luke, Han also receives a medal from Princess Leia.

3. **Explain the role destiny and free will play in the lives of the characters.**

The mystical force in *Star Wars* seems to represent a combination of religion, faith, and destiny. It seems that the character's actions are influenced by their destiny, but they make decisions of their own free will. Ben tells Luke that a Jedi can feel the force. Luke asks if that means that the force controls your actions. Ben answers, "Partially, but it also obeys your commands." Han Solo laughs at the idea of a mystical force that controls one's destiny. When Luke demonstrates his skill with the light saber, Han says it is just luck. Ben retorts that there is no such thing as luck. When Luke asks to accompany Ben to battle Darth Vader, Ben tells him to stay with the droids, because "your destiny lies in a different path from mine." Even evil Vader respects the power of the force. He tells the military members of the empire that they should not underestimate the power of the force. When Vader sees Luke's prowess in battle, he proclaims that he can see that the force is strong with him. When Luke expresses disappointment that Han will not stay and fight with them, Leia tells Luke that Han has to follow his own path and that no one can choose it for him. Of course Han leaves, but then returns of his own free will. Luke is a good and brave pilot, but in the final battle, he trusts in the force to help him win. He does so, and he is victorious. However, it is the last-minute help by Han Solo that enables Luke to defeat the empire fighters.

26. Tangled

Film Data

Year: 2010

Director: Nathan Greno and Byron Howard

Length: 100 minutes

Rated: PG

Characters/Actors

Rapunzel (voice):   Mandy Moore

Flynn Rider (voice):   Zachary Levi

Mother Gothel (voice):   Donna Murphy

Stabbington Brother (voice): Ron Perlman

Captain of the Guard (voice): M. C. Gainey

Big Nose Thug (voice):   Jeffrey Tambor

Hook Hand Thug (voice):   Brad Garrett

Connection to Chapters

Chapter 34. Applying Theory: How to Perform a Jungian Analysis

Chapter 37. Germany: Grimms' *Household Tales*

Recommended Scenes

The scene of Mother Gothel singing about why Rapunzel cannot ever leave occurs at 00:13:04 through 00:15:35.

The scene of Mother Gothel and Rapunzel hugging occurs at 00:24:20.

The scene of Rapunzel making the deal with Flynn and then singing about seeing the world occurs at 00:28:31 through 00:30:28.

The scene of Rapunzel realizing her dream and seeing the lanterns occurs at 01:06:42.

The scene of the final confrontation between Rapunzel and Mother Gothel occurs from 01:15:30 through 01:19:00.

The scene of Flynn cutting Rapunzel's hair and then being healed by her tears occurs at 01:24:30.

The scene of Rapunzel being reunited with her real parents and living happily ever after occurs at 01:28:47.

Instructor Viewing Information

Tangled is very loosely based on the Grimm Brothers' *Rapunzel,* even though the film gives Jacob and Wilhelm Grimm a screenwriting credit along with Dan Fogelman. *Tangled* is a Disney musical with music composed by Alan Menken. The film's characters are voiced by pop star Mandy Moore, Broadway star Donna Murphy, and television star Zach Levi. The film changes some key elements to make the tale more palatable for children, but students may still enjoy the humor in this animated tale. *Tangled* should be a good way to discuss Otto Rank's ideas about the family romance, as well as a good way to start a discussion of household tales and Jungian analysis of household tales.

Synopsis

Mother Gothel (Murphy) finds a magical flower with healing powers. She uses it to keep herself young. Later, the flower is found to heal a Queen who is ill and in childbirth. The Queen gives birth to Rapunzel (Moore), whose hair glows and heals, but will lose its magic if cut. Mother Gothel kidnaps the baby and raises Rapunzel as her daughter. She never cuts Rapunzel's hair and keeps her locked from the world in a tower. Every year on her birthday, the King and Queen release lanterns of light, hoping the lost princess will return. Rapunzel watches the lights and wants to see them on her eighteenth birthday. The Queen refuses. When a thief named Flynn (Levi) steals a tiara from the castle, he hides in the tower. Rapunzel hits him with a frying pan and gets the tiara. She makes a deal with Flynn to exchange the tiara for a chance to see the lights. They escape, have adventures, and begin to have romantic feelings for each other. Eventually Gothel captures Rapunzel and Flynn. Rapunzel realizes that she is the real princess and that Gothel kidnapped her. She says that if Gothel spares Flynn's life, she will stay with Gothel forever. Before Rapunzel can heal Flynn with her hair, Flynn cuts it. Gothel grows old and dies and Rapunzel heals Flynn. Rapunzel is reunited with her parents and takes her rightful place as the princess. She marries Flynn, and all live happily in the kingdom.

Discussion Questions

1. **Explain how the film illustrates the maturation and initiation cycle, as well as Rank's ideas of the family romance.**

In the beginning of the film, Mother Gothel steals Rapunzel from her real parents, the king and queen. Mother Gothel then locks Rapunzel in a tower and raises Rapunzel as her own daughter. Mother Gothel forces Rapunzel to stays in the tower, far from her real home. She uses Rapunzel's hair to keep her young. Although she says she loves Rapunzel, Mother Gothel teases and insults her and tries to erode Rapunzel's self-confidence. Rapunzel convinces a thief named Flynn to leave the tower with her. On several occasions, she uses the natural power of her hair, as both a light and a lasso, to help escape danger. Rapunzel learns the truth about her real parents, the king and queen. She confronts Mother Gothel with the truth. Flynn helps her defeat Mother Gothel. Even though Flynn cuts Rapunzel's hair, her tears heal Flynn. At the end of the film, Rapunzel is reunited with her parents, and she assumes her rightful place as princess. We are told that when it is her turn to rule the kingdom, she does so as wisely as her parents.

2. **Explain how the film changes the tale to reflect contemporary values.**

The contemporary values of individuality and female independence are also present here. Rapunzel is shown to be a spirited and spunky young woman. When she hits intruder Flynn with a frying pan and locks him in her closet, she is proud. Rapunzel believes that this will show her mother that she can take care of herself in the outside world. Rapunzel even sings about wanting to leave home and experience the world. In the film, Flynn is a common thief, not a prince. This places more emphasis on Rapunzel's power. Flynn helps Rapunzel defeat Mother Gothel, but she also talks their way out of trouble in a tavern. Rapunzel shows how resourceful she is when she finds ways to use her hair to combat her enemies. A more contemporary, positive view of the world is also shown here. Mother Gothel frequently tells Rapunzel that the world is a dangerous place filled with horrible and selfish people. At the end of the film, Rapunzel stands up to Mother Gothel and tells her that she is wrong about the world. Rapunzel's positive view of the world is reinforced by the film's ending. Rapunzel is reunited with her real parents, Flynn and Rapunzel and get married, Rapunzel rules wisely, and all live happily ever after.

3. **Describe how the film portrays changing ideas of parent/child relationships.**

The contemporary idea of the quintessential protective mother is shown here. Mother Gothel never physically harms Rapunzel, but she convinces Rapunzel that she is too innocent and fragile for the outside world. She wants Rapunzel to stay with her forever. Mother Gothel wants to hold on to her youth with the magical properties of Rapunzel's hair, in effect staying young by keeping her child with her forever. Mother Gothel and Rapunzel hug and proclaim their love for each other. Mother Gothel makes Rapunzel's favorite foods. But Mother Gothel tries to make Rapunzel feel bad about herself by insulting her and then saying that she is only kidding. She distorts the truth about Flynn to keep Rapunzel home with her. In this film, the evil fake mother is not physically abusive, but controlling and overprotective.

27. Thor

Film Data

Year: 2011

Director: Kenneth Branagh

Length: 115 minutes

Rated: PG-13

Characters/Actors

Chris Hemsworth: Thor

Natalie Portman: Jane Foster

Tom Hiddleston: Loki

Anthony Hopkins: Odin

Stellan Skarsgård: Erik Selvig

Kat Dennings: Darcy Lewis

Clark Gregg: Agent Coulson

Idris Elba: Heimdall

Colm Feore: King Laufey

Connection to Chapters

Chapter 19. Icelandic/Norse: *Prose Edda*

Chapter 31. Icelandic/Norse: The Rituals of Iceland (H. R. E. Davidson)

Recommended Scenes

The scene of Odin telling Thor he is thinking like a warrior occurs at 00:012:15.

The scene of Loki and Thor battling the frost giants occurs at 00:17:36 through 00:22:28.

The scene of Odin banishing Thor occurs at 00:26:28 through 00:29:41.

The scene of the gods talking about Loki being mischievous occurs at 00:39:04.

The scene of Thor trying to retrieve his hammer at the military facility occurs at 00:54:43 through 00:58:40.

The scene of Loki lying to Thor on earth occurs at 01:04:43.

The scene of Thor asking Loki to spare innocent lives and then retrieving his hammer and fighting the metal giant occurs at 01:25:00 through 01:29:41.

The scene of the final battle between Thor and Loki occurs at 01:36:00.

Instructor Viewing Information

Thor is based on the Marvel comic book by Stan Lee. The film imagines the attractive and strong Thor (Hemsworth) to be somewhat of a superhero, who is banished to earth from Asgard. The film alternates scenes in Asgard with scenes on modern-day earth. Thor is also treated with humor in the scenes on earth. Although the film changes many aspects of the myth of Thor, *Thor* provides some good examples of Thor's better-known characteristics. Students may be familiar with this film, and will certainly enjoy the special effects and actions sequences. *Thor* should provide an enjoyable way to discuss the Thor, Odin, Loki, Asgard, and the Norse gods.

Synopsis

Thor is expelled from Asgard by Odin (Hopkins), in part due to the trickery of Loki (Hiddleston). Thor crashes to earth and is found by scientists Jane (Portman), Erik (Skarsgård), and Darcy (Dennings). Thor is now human. Jane helps Thor in his quest to retrieve his hammer, the Mjollnir, and wants Thor to help with her research. The two develop romantic feelings for each other. On Asgard, Loki's machinations place him in charge while Odin is seriously ill. Loki attempts to strand Thor on earth and sends a metal giant to kill him. Thor fights the giant and retrieves his hammer and saves Jane and the other humans. Thor learns the truth about Loki and is able to return to Asgard. Odin is saved and Thor saves the frost giants from Loki's plan to destroy them. But in doing so, Thor must destroy the Bifrost Bridge, which is also the bridge to earth. Thor and Loki fight, and Loki falls to earth. The film ends with reconciliation between Odin and Thor, and Thor is made ruler. Thor misses Jane, but is told that on earth, Jane continues to search for him.

Discussion Questions

1. Explain how the film portrays the transcendence and immanence of Odin and Thor.

Although Odin is shown to be the ruler of Asgard, in this film he is portrayed as more of a wise leader than a violent and cunning ruler. At first glance, he may seem transcendent, as he is never shown visiting earth and seems to have no relationship with mortals. But in the beginning of the film, Odin makes it clear that he wishes to protect mortals and explains this in a voiceover. In *Thor,* Thor spends much of the film on earth with mortals. In fact, Thor is made mortal when he is banished. Thor shows that he is approachable by getting to know Jane and Erik. He shows his rough and crude manners when he wolfs down breakfast, smashes a coffee cup, and gets drunk with Erik. He further shows his rough manners and interest in everyday human activities when he carries Erik home after they drink together. Thor laughingly tells Jane that Erik made him proud. Even after Thor returns to being a god, he still in interested in human activities, and still loves Jane, a mortal.

2. Describe how the film shows Thor to be both fallible and heroic.

In this film, Thor is very much the strong and powerful figure one would expect. He also wields his weapon, the Mjollnir, which returns to him after he throws it. The film also shows Thor to be a champion of Asgard. When Asgard is attacked, Thor wants to cross the Bifrost Bridge to retaliate against the frost giants. Odin disagrees, and tells Thor that he is thinking like a warrior, rather than a future ruler. Thor also show his strength and warrior nature when he punches his way into a secure government compound to retrieve the Mjollnir. Thor also shows a voracious appetite for food and drink when he eats with Jane at the diner and drinks in a bar with Erik. But in *Thor,* details of the myth are altered to show Thor developing and changing. When Odin banishes Thor and takes the Mjollnir, Odin proclaims that whoever holds the hammer and is worthy shall possess the power of Thor. When Thor first tries to retrieve the hammer, he cannot lift it. But through the course of the film, Thor changes. He learns to be polite and helps Jane and Erik. But Thor shows how much he has changed when he fights the metal giant sent by Loki. Even though he is human, Thor sends his friends away and fights. He then asks Loki to spare innocent lives and take his life instead. In is then when Thor is worthy enough for the hammer to return to him. Thor is a god again. When Thor returns to Asgard, he destroys the Bifrost Bridge to stop Loki from destroying the race of frost giants. By doing this, he knows that he may never be able to return to earth and see Jane. When Loki questions Thor's actions, Thor explains that he has changed. Thor now sees that there is a time to avoid violence. At the end of the film, Thor no longer argues with Odin. He is humble. Odin tells Thor that he will be a good ruler.

3. **Describe how the film portrays Loki as a trickster.**

In this film, Loki is Thor's brother. However, the film takes the idea that Loki is the son of a giant and changes it. Here, Loki is the son of King Laufey (Feore), a frost giant. Odin stole baby Loki and raised him as his own son. At the start of the film, Loki is shown to be socializing with Thor and his god friends in Asgard. After Thor has been banished from Asgard, Thor's friends wonder if Loki is to blame. They acknowledge that he has always been mischievous, but involvement here would be very different from mischief. Loki here is a bit of villain, although he uses tricks and duplicity. Loki endangers Asgard so he can get credit for saving the day. He lies to Thor about Odin being dead and their mother being angry. Loki shows that he is more villain than trickster when he tries to kill Thor and then tries to kill the race of frost giants. But at the end of the film, Loki plays his final trick. He appears to kill himself as he careens off the Bifrost Bridge to earth. However, after the film's final credits, we see him in a future scene on earth, whispering in Erik's ear.

28. The Tree of Life

Film Data

Year: 2011

Director: Terrence Malick

Length: 139 minutes

Rated: PG-13

Characters/Actors

Brad Pitt: Mr. O'Brien

Sean Penn: Jack

Jessica Chastain: Mrs. O'Brien

Hunter McCracken: Young Jack

Laramie Eppler: R.L.

Tye Sheridan: Steve

Connection to Chapters

Part IIA. Myths of Creation and Destruction—Creation: Introductory Overview

Chapter 5. The Bible: Genesis (Creation)

Recommended Scenes

The scene of Mrs. O'Brien talking about nature and grace occurs at 00:02:05 through 00:04:14.

The scene of the creation of the world occurs at 00:19:39 through 00:36:59.

The scene of Mr. O'Brien giving his sons advice occurs at 00:59:55 through 01:01:11.

The scene of the end of time and the characters walking together on the beach occurs at 02:01:50 through 02:11:59.

Instructor Viewing Information

The Tree of Life mixes pensive meditations on the meaning of life with scenes of a 1950s childhood, interwoven with scenes of the creation and destruction of the world. The film is visually stunning, and tells some of its story with little accompanying dialogue. While some students may appreciate the film, others may find it taxing. The nonlinear plot and fragmented scenes may cause some students to find the film inaccessible and difficult to understand. Some introduction and preparation for the film will be needed. The film features excellent performances, and students will most likely be familiar with actors Brad Pitt and Sean Penn. *The Tree of Life* should provide an excellent way to discuss creation and the relevance of creation myths for contemporary audiences.

Synopsis

The film begins with young Mrs. O'Brien (Chastain) learning that her nineteen-year-old son has been killed. Neighbors offer the grieving parents sympathy. The scene then shifts to middle-aged Jack O'Brien (Penn) in his successful job in a high-rise building. He seems unhappy as he thinks about his dead brother and his childhood. Most of the film recounts scenes from Jack's childhood in suburban Texans in the 1950s. Young Jack (McCracken) and his brothers R.L. (Eppler) and Steve (Sheridan) spend long days playing outside. They sometimes hear their parents argue through open windows. Their mother is loving and sweet, but their father, Mr. O'Brien (Pitt), is strict and sometimes seems abusive. Mr. O'Brien works in a plant, but yearned to be a musician in his youth. He spends his free time patenting and trying to sell his numerous inventions. Jack, who is the oldest brother, misbehaves and frequently clashes with his stern father. Near the end of the film, the plant employing Mr. O'Brien closes and the family sadly leaves their home. Interspersed with the scenes of Jack's childhood are scenes of a pensive adult Jack at home and at work. We also see scenes that appear to show the universe being created. Over some of these scenes are whispered musings from Mrs. O'Brien, young Jack, and the adult Jack. The characters wonder about God, suffering, love, and the meaning of the life. The film ends with a vision of an afterlife where adult Jack meets his younger self, his brothers as children, and his parents as they looked in his childhood. They embrace and seem happy, and others join them as they walk together on a beach.

Discussion Questions

1. **Describe the way creation myths are referred to in the film.**

Before the film begins we see the text of a quote from the Book of Job. In this quote, God asks where Job was when He created the world. The film begins and ends with a small spark of life. The stories of the O'Briens are interrupted by a sequence depicting the creation of the universe. The film shows a view of creation that could be explained by the scientific Big Bang theory, but could also support some of the accounts of biblical creation in Genesis. The film shows many steps in the creation process such as a dark and formless void and then a fiery explosion. We also see darkness and then stars, the beginning of light and what seems to be a separation between earth and sky and land and water. Later, *The Tree of Life* shows the beginning of life starting with microscopic cells, jellyfish, and large sea creatures. The sequence ends with smaller dinosaurs interacting with each other. Over some of these sequences we hear the characters whisper questions about the nature of their existence. The characters also refer to the God of the Bible in these whispered questions.

2. **Explain how the film refers to the biblical creation story in Genesis.**

The title of the film, *The Tree of Life,* refers to the account of Adam and Eve in the Garden of Eden described in the J-E creation account in Genesis. In this version, the Tree of Life and the Tree of Knowledge of Good and Evil are forbidden. In the film, Mrs. O'Brien recounts that the nuns taught her two choices for living one's life. Mrs. O'Brien explains the difference between the way of grace and the way of nature. According to Mrs. O'Brien, grace does not try to please itself and can accept insults and injuries. Nature only tries to please itself and lords it over others. This describes the struggle Jack faces about his life. He sees his mother and father at war in himself. Mrs. O'Brien tells her sons that without love, life goes by in an instant. She wants them to try to help each other. Mr. O'Brien tells his sons that their mother is naive. He teaches the boys to fight and tells them they need to be fierce to get ahead in life. Jack, Mr. O'Brien, and Mrs. O'Brien pray before meals and attend church. They often talk to God and believe in a deity who created the world has control over the lives of humans. Jack, both as a child and as an adult, struggles to find meaning in the world and his life.

3. **Describe how the film uses details of both the character's daily lives and their view of creation to show their priorities.**

Although the characters in the film have different views on life, God is important in their daily lives. The extended scene of creation shown with the whispered questions about life

112

shows the way the characters strive to find their place in the larger plan. They all need to believe in a God who created the world. They need to believe in a divine entity to give meaning to otherwise random events. Mrs. O'Brien points to the sky and tells her sons that the sky is where God lives. When young Jack sees a child drown in a pool, he wonders if the child was punished for being bad. Later, young Jack prays to God and asks God to kill his father. When the O'Briens learn of their son's death, Mr. O'Brien tries to comfort his wife by telling her that now their son is in God's hand. Mrs. O'Brien responds that their son was always in God's hands. The film contains many beautiful shots of trees, flowers, and bodies of water, fully emphasizing nature's beauty and what the characters see as the beauty of God's creation. Mrs. O'Brien talks about the importance of appreciating the beauty that is all around you. The way the O'Briens can make sense of their son's death is by believing in a God who is responsible for creating the world. At the end of the film, Mr. O'Brien loses his job and changes his philosophy of life. He laments not noticing the glory of the beauty around him, and says that by not appreciating it, he dishonored it. His belief allows him to try to apologize to Jack. The film ends with adult Jack in an elevator. It seems he has a vision of sorts. He prays that God "keep us and guide us to the end of time." The scenes underneath this suggest the end of time, or time when the world has ended. Jack sees a barren landscape where his family and others recognize and embrace each other, and then walk on a beach. The scene suggests love, forgiveness, and acceptance. The film ends with the same spark of light that began the film. The characters see themselves as connected to all in the universe through a larger plan.

29. Troy

Film Data

Year: 2004

Director: Wolfgang Petersen

Length: 163 minutes

Rated: R

Characters/Actors

Brad Pitt: Achilles

Brian Cox: Agamemnon

Brendan Gleeson: Menelaus

Diane Kruger: Helen

Eric Bana: Hector

Orlando Bloom: Paris

Peter O'Toole: Priam

Saffron Burrows: Andromache

Rose Byrne: Briseis

Garrett Hedlund: Patroclus

Connection to Chapters

Chapter 1. What Is Myth?

Chapter 44. Poetry and Myth

Recommended Scenes

The scene of Achilles talking to his mother occurs at 00:24:53 through 00:26:40.

The scene of Achilles desecrating the temple and discussing immortality with Hector occurs at 00:44:13 through 00:48:05.

The scene of Achilles and Briseis discussing the gods occurs at 01:29:30 through 01:31:17.

The scene of the final battle between Hector and Achilles occurs at 01:57:23 through 02:02:33.

The scene of Priam asking Achilles for Hector's corpse occurs at 02:07:33.

The scene of the Trojan horse and ensuing battle begins at 02:17:28.

Instructor Viewing Information

Troy is big-budget sprawling adventure and romance film that tells the story of the Trojan War. The film credits Homer along with screenwriter David Benioff for the characters and story. Of course, the filmmakers changed some of the details of the myth. For example, Menelaus and Agamemnon are both killed in the film, but survive in the myth. (See Kim Shahabudin's article "From Greek Myth to Hollywood Story," which appears in Martin M. Winkler's anthology *Troy from Homer's* Iliad *to Hollywood Epic,* p. 112.) The film contains brief nudity and violence. Some may find *Troy* a bit bloated and long, but students should enjoy the large-scale battle scenes. The film provides an interesting way to discuss contemporary film adaptations of myths. *Troy* also provides an interesting and enjoyable way to discuss the role of the gods in the lives of mortals, as well as the importance of immortality for these characters.

Synopsis

While Paris (Bloom) and Hector (Bana) are in Sparta for peace negotiations with King Menelaus (Gleeson), Paris and Helen (Kruger), the king's wife, fall in love. When Paris and Helen leave together, an angry Menelaus and his war-mongering brother King Agamemnon (Cox) prepare to attack Troy. Achilles (Pitt) is Agamemnon's best warrior, but they have a strained relationship. Achilles reluctantly agrees to fight. Troy suffers losses, and Briseis (Byrne), who is cousin to Paris and Hector, is taken prisoner by Achilles. Paris challenges Menelaus to a fight in order to resolve the dispute. Paris does not fight well and loses, but Hector protects his brother by killing Menelaus. Achilles and Briseis develop romantic feelings for each other, and Achilles orders his army to leave Troy. But Achilles' young cousin Patroclus (Hedlund) dresses in Achilles' armor and attacks Troy. Hector kills Patroclus, thinking he is Achilles. An enraged Achilles fights Hector and kills him. Achilles allows King Priam (O'Toole) to bury his son Hector and allows

Briseis to return to Troy. Agamemnon's army and Achilles hide in a large model of a horse and burn Troy. Agamemnon threatens Briseis, but Briseis kills him. Achilles then comes to her rescue and helps Briseis escape. Paris then shoots Achilles in the heel and kills him. Achilles and Briseis kiss goodbye as he dies, and then Briseis escapes with Paris and Helen.

Discussion Questions

1. **Explain how the characters in the film view human freedom and the role of the gods.**

    Most of the characters in the film ask the gods to be with them in battle, and credit the gods with their victories. Achilles and Hector are the two characters in the film who express doubt about the power of the gods. Achilles gives his men permission to loot a Trojan temple, but one of his men hesitates, saying that Apollo sees all. Briseis tells Achilles that Apollo will avenge the death of his priests, but Achilles counters that the gods fear him. He also tells Briseis that he has seen the gods. Later, a high priest tells King Priam that the gods sent birds as a sign that that Trojans will win the war. Hector does not believe the signs. He tells his father that although he has always honored the gods, the sight of Achilles desecrating the temple filled him with doubt. He wonders why the gods did not intervene. Hector believes men must win the war without the help of gods. Achilles and Briseis debate the role of the gods in the lives of mortals. Achilles wonders how the pacifist Briseis can love the god of war. She believes all the gods must be respected. Achilles argues that the gods envy mortals their mortality. Achilles says that mortality makes every moment more beautiful. Achilles and Hector believe in the gods, but they see humans as free to make their own choices.

2. **Describe how the characters in the film view the importance of eternal fame and mortal lives.**

    Achilles and Hector exemplify two opposite positions on the importance of eternal fame. In the beginning of the film, a little boy tells Achilles that he cannot imagine fighting such fearsome opponents. "That is why no one will remember your name," replies Achilles. Before leaving for Troy, Achilles has a conversation with his mother. She tells him he has two choices for his life. He can stay and have a happy marriage and family, and his family will praise him. But after his grandchildren die, no one will remember the name Achilles. She goes on to say that if he fights in Troy, people will remember his name for thousands of years, but she will never see her son again. Achilles' mother explains that glory and doom go hand in hand. When Achilles first meets Hector, Achilles tells him that people will be talking about their war for thousands of years.

116

Hector says that by then their "bones will be dust." Achilles is moody and introspective, and does not seem to really enjoy fighting. He wants immortality, but he does not seem to really enjoy his life until he meets Briseis. Hector lives in the present. He has a happy marriage with Andromache (Burrows) and loves his infant son. Hector tells his wife that he wants to watch his son grow up. Hector does not crave immortality; he wants to live his happy mortal life. He is Troy's best warrior, but he does not enjoy killing. Hector fights because he feels it is the right thing to do. He is loyal to his father, brother, and country.

3. **Explain how the film interprets the myth to reflect the changing tastes and expectations of a contemporary audience.**

Troy tells the story of the mostly sympathetic mortal characters. The gods are referred to often by the characters, but the film does not show any individual gods. In the film, Helen and Paris have a torrid love affair. She wants to go to Troy with her lover. No woman in the film is forced to do anything against her will. Even when Achilles captures Briseis, he treats her with respect. Hector is also loving and kind to his wife. Contemporary audiences expect to see woman treated with respect, even in times when this would not have been the case. Paris, Hector, and Achilles have long, thoughtful discussions with Helen, Andromache, and Briseis. Although Hector and Achilles are skilled warriors, they are complex people with nuanced emotions. Audiences today would empathize with men who act this way. Men who are nothing more than savage warriors might not be sympathetic to contemporary audiences. When King Priam and Paris prepare for battle, Paris tries to explain the depths of his love for Helen. King Priam says that love is a better reason for war than many other reasons. The focus on the love between Paris and Helen makes the Trojans more sympathetic characters.

30. Twilight

Film Data

Year: 2008

Director: Catherine Hardwicke

Length: 122 minutes

Rated: PG-13

Characters/Actors

Kristen Stewart: Bella Swan

Robert Pattinson: Edward Cullen

Billy Burke: Charlie Swan

Taylor Lautner: Jacob Black

Rachelle Lefevre: Victoria

Peter Facinelli: Dr. Carlisle Cullen

Sarah Clarke: Renée

Cam Gigandet: James

Connection to Chapters

Chapter 43. The Vampire as Hero: Tales of the Undead in a Contemporary Context

Recommended Scenes

The scene of Edward stopping a car from hitting Bella occurs at 00:21:13.

The scene of Edward rescuing Bella from a gang of predatory boys and then telling Bella he feels protective toward her occurs at 00:39:38 through 00:44:30.

The scene of Bella and Edward discussing his vampire urges and self-control occurs at 00:50:20 through 00:56:05.

The scene of Edward telling Bella about the temptation of human blood occurs at 00:59:47.

The scene Edward stopping himself from having sex with Bella occurs at 01:15:01 through 01:16:09.

The scene of Carlisle telling his family to protect Bella occurs at 01:30:08.

The scene of Edward sucking the venom from Bella's blood occurs at 01:45:00.

Instructor Viewing Information

Twilight is the first in the series of films based on Stephenie Meyer's best-selling novels. Students should be familiar with the characters and actors in the film. Some students will be fans of the series and others may view *Twilight* with disdain, but they should enjoy discussing this popular film. Although the film continues with the conservative ideologies found in the novels, *Twilight* provides a good way to begin a discussion of vampires. *Twilight* provides an excellent way to examine the reasons for the popularity of vampires, the ideas of Melanie Klein, and the values advanced in this film.

Synopsis

When her mother Renée (Clarke) goes on the road with her husband, Bella (Stewart), a high school student, moves to Forks, Washington, to live with her father, Charlie (Burke). Moping Bella meets fellow student Edward Cullen (Pattinson) and although he pretends to dislike her, their mutual attraction is obvious. Edward displays unusual strength when he pushes Bella out of the path of an oncoming car and saves her from attack by a gang of predatory boys. Bella realizes that something is not right with Edward and his mysterious family, but does not figure out that he is a vampire until halfway through the film. Edward tells her that he and his family only eat animals, but he is tempted by Bella's blood, and cannot trust himself to get too close to her. But they begin to date and Edward introduces Bella to his family. They encounter another clan of vampires who have been killing people in Forks. These vampires are led by Victoria (Lefevre) and James (Gigandet). When tracker James gets Bella's scent, Bella must leave town. Edward's family helps her, but James threatens Bella's mother and captures Bella. Edward and his family come to the rescue and save Bella's life. Bella recovers from her injuries and tells her mother she wants to remain in Forks with her father. The film ends with Edward and Bella at the prom. Bella wants Edward to turn her into a vampire so they can be together forever. Edward refuses for now, and the film ends with the couple dancing.

Discussion Questions

1. **Explain how the film shows Melanie Klein's ideas about "inappropriate mothering."**

At the start of the film, Bella affectionately refers to her mother as "harebrained." Although they seem to have a warm relationship, we learn that Bella's mother wants to accompany her husband, whose career as a minor league baseball player forces him to travel. Bella tells Edward that when she saw her mother was unhappy being separated from her husband, Bella volunteered to live with her father in Forks. "So now you are unhappy," counters Edward. In a sense, Bella's mother chose her husband over Bella. We also learn that Bella's mother was the one to end the marriage to Bella's father. Bella is assuming the maternal role in her relationship with her mother. In fact, Bella is willing to trade her own life to save her mother's life, when she is threatened by James. Bella also runs away to protect her father from James. Bella appears to be looking to Edward and Edward's family to compensate for her own deficient family. When Edward invites Bella to meet his family, they enthusiastically prepare a home-cooked meal in their lovely home, despite the fact that they do not eat food. This is very different than the diner fare Bella and Charlie regularly consume for dinner. After Edward saves Bella's life, he tells her that he feels protective of her. When Bella's life is threatened by James, Dr. Carlisle Cullen (Facinelli) tells the other Cullens that Bella is now part of their family and "we protect our family." At the same time, Bella is unable to reach her mother on the telephone. Bella, who does not have a mother who really protects her, is drawn to Edward and his family, who very much want to protect her. Edward tells Bella that she is his life now. Bella seem to have found what she lacked in her own mother, someone to put her first.

2. **Describe how the film portrays men and women struggling with greedy and powerful aspects of their world and their own nature.**

Edward describes himself as a "vegetarian" because he does not drink the blood of humans, and only drinks the blood of animals. Bella is a vegetarian and chides her father for eating meat. Edward tells Bella that for a vampire, eating animal blood is like humans eating tofu. It sustains you but you never feel satisfied. Skinny Bella, who eats ravioli and garden burgers, does not comment. Both control their appetites for food. Likewise, Edward tells Bella that her scent is too much for him. He tells her she should not trust him, because he may not be able to control himself, as once a vampire tastes human blood, it is difficult to stop. When they kiss on her bed, Edward jumps off the bed and yells, "Stop." Edward tells Bella that he is stronger than he thought. Bella replies that she wishes she could say the same. Here, Edward controls both his appetite for blood and his appetite for sex. Bella has trouble controlling her desire to have sex with Edward, but Edward helps her control her desire. When James attacks Bella, Edward must suck the venom out of her blood in order to save her life. Edward tells Carlisle that he is afraid if he does so, he will not be able to stop sucking Bella's blood. But again, Edward manages to control himself. In *Twilight* denial and self-control are the solution to the greed.

3. **Explain how the film shows that Bella's encounters with vampires allow her to reshape her world.**

Bella is gloomy and unhappy when she moves to Forks. Her mother has gone away and she must live with a father she does not know very well. Charlie appears to be a concerned father as he gives her a truck and advises her to use pepper spray, but Bella and Charlie struggle to define their father/daughter relationship. As Bella gets to know the Cullens, she sees what the family she craves might look like. As Bella becomes a part of this vampire family, she redefines her relationship with her own family. She realizes that her father is important to her and that she enjoys living with him. At the end of the film, she refuses her mother's offer to return home. Although she wants to stay in Forks with Edward, she also wants to continue living with her father. Bella also realizes that she loves Edward, and wants him to make her a vampire. Although he refuses, the films ends with Bella saying that she will not give in on this and that she knows what she wants. Bella has a life in a new town, friends, a renewed relationship with her father and love. She has reshaped her world and reached a place of illumination. She understands what she wants from life.

31. Whale Rider

Film Data

Year: 2002

Director: Niki Caro

Length: 101 minutes

Rated: PG-13

Characters/Actors

Keisha Castle-Hughes:	Paikea
Rawiri Paratene:	Koro
Vicky Haughton:	Nanny Flowers
Cliff Curtis:	Porourangi
Grant Roa:	Uncle Rawiri

Connection to Chapters

Chapter 15. Theory: Joseph Campbell, *The Hero with a Thousand Faces* (Dave Whomsley)

Chapter 34. Applying Theory: How to Perform a Jungian Analysis

Recommended Scenes

The scene of Koro and Porourangi arguing about the obligations of destiny occurs at 00:22:11 through 00:24:10.

The scene of Porourangi explaining Koro and traditions to Pai occurs at 00:25:30 through 00:27:16.

The scene of Uncle Rawiri training Pai occurs at 00:46:20 through 00:47:40.

The scene of Pai giving a speech about her grandfather occurs at 01:11:40 through 01:15:48.

The scene of Pai riding the whale occurs at 01:25:38 through 01:31:40.

The scene of Koro accepting Pai, the ceremony, and the resolution of the story occurs at 01:33:20 through the end of the film.

Instructor Viewing Information

Whale Rider was shot on the New Zealand island where it takes places. The film features a much-acclaimed performance from then-eleven-year-old Keisha Castle-Hughes. While this film is about a child, this is not a children's film. Students should enjoy the plot, humor, and interesting setting in this wonderful film. *Whale Rider* provides an excellent example of a young girl on a hero's quest. The film should also provide an enjoyable and interesting way to discuss the ideas of Joseph Campbell, as well as Jung's archetypes. *Whale Rider* tells a story of the relevance of old myths to a present-day culture, and should spark a lively discussion of these ideas.

Synopsis

The film is set in present-day New Zealand. A flashback voiced by young Pai (Castle-Hughes) tells us that Pai's mother died in childbirth, as did her twin brother. Pai is descended from a line of Maori chiefs, dating back to the first ancestor Paikea. Legend has it that Paikea rode on a whale from another island. The title of chief is passed through firstborn sons, and Pai's dead brother was thought to be the next in line after Pai's father. Overcome with sadness, Pai's father, Porourani (Curtis), leaves the island to be an artist. He does not wish to be the next chief, even though he would be next in line. Pai is raised by her grandmother Nanny Flowers (Haughton) and her grandfather Koro (Paratene). They love her, but Koro wishes she were a boy. When Koro feels the village needs a new chief, he trains all the firstborn boys in the old ways. Pai wants to attend but it is forbidden for girls. She spies and learns on her own, and shows both aptitude and passion. Pai angers Koro, but she continues to love him. Pai turns down the chance to leave with her father because she feels she must stay in her village. Signs point to Pai as the new chief, but Koro refuses to believe the new chief could be a girl. When Pai risks her life by riding a beached whale to sea, Koro finally accepts her as the new leader. The film ends with the entire village, including the returning Porourangi, happily celebrating together in a colorful religious ceremony. Pai has unified all in the village. In a voiceover she stated that she knows her people will continue on.

Discussion Questions

1. **Explain how in the film Pai takes some of the steps in the hero's journey as outlined by Campbell.**

In synthesizing the ideas of both Otto Rank and Carl Jung, Campbell emphasized the importance of both male and female figures in the hero's adventure. Although Campbell's analysis envisioned a male hero, it is instructive to examine the way contemporary female hero figures may follow some of these same patterns. Campbell bases his ideas on a gendered, Freudian model: the male hero fights a (same-sex) father figure and resists a(n) (opposite-sex) temptress and unites with a(n) (opposite-sex) goddess. It would stand to reason that these genders would be reversed if the hero is female. However, Pai seems to inherit the characteristics of a male hero, as her main struggle is with her grandfather Koro, and her main inspiration is her grandmother Nanny Flowers. When Pai is born, Porourani names her Paikea, after their first ancestor. He does this despite strong objections from Koro. Although Porourani has no interest in assuming his place as chief, he wants to pass his heritage to his daughter. In a sense, destiny has called Pai. But Pai is passionate about her heritage and yearns to learn. Despite opposition from Koro, she insists on learning the ancient ways, by asking questions and spying on Koro training the boys. Pai voluntarily answers the call to adventure. Pai has two protective figures that advise and teach her. Her grandmother teaches her the ancient prayers and advises her to seek out her uncle. Her grandmother also provides love and a nurturing environment. Pai learns from her grandmother that Pai's out-of-shape Uncle Rawiri (Roa) was a champion in the traditional fighting stick competition. While Koro trains the boys to use the stick, Uncle Rawiri trains Pai. Pai has two trials involving water. Koro takes the boys he has been training to deeper water. He throws his prized whale tooth necklace into the sea, saying that the true chief must pass the test of retrieving the whale tooth. None of the boys can find it. Later Pai asks Rawiri to take her in a boat to the spot where Koro threw the whale tooth. Pai says she will find it, and she does. When several whales wash up on shore, Koro sees it as a bad sign and blames Pai. The village works together to get the largest whale back in the water. But Pai accomplishes this when she rides the whale to sea. While not technically in the belly of the whale, Pai is on the whale and dragged under water. She believes in what she is doing and states that she is not afraid to die. Pai survives and Koro stays by her bedside. He refers to her as a wise leader and asks her for forgiveness. Pai overcomes the father figure, achieving "father atonement" on a symbolic level. While she always loved her grandfather, he opposed her desire to learn and resented the fact that she was born female. At the end of the film, he embraces her as a leader of their people. When she awakens, she sees that Koro has places the whale necklace around her neck. This is a symbol of her quest and her new status as leader.

2. **Describe how Pai's journey in the film is a spiritual quest.**

Pai's spiritual quest is to retain the old ways and combine them with new and modern ideas. Her grandfather blamed the birth of a female child (Pai) for all that was wrong in the village. Koro saw his son leaving the island and his heritage. Koro was afraid the old ways were dying and would be forgotten. But Pai loves the old stories and prayers. Her actions convince Koro that Pai, a female, is their new leader. After Pai recovers from her whale ride, the community comes together and celebrates. Pai's father returns with his pregnant girlfriend and finishes building the boat he long ago abandoned. Pai and her family, along with the entire community, joyfully participate in an ancient ceremony. They dance, chant, and ride the boat in the sea. Pai has reawakened interest and passion in the old traditions. The film ends with Pai reflecting on her future. She says that she is not a prophet, but she knows that her people will keep going forward together, using all of their strengths.

3. **Describe how the film uses Jung's archetypes of animus, shadow, and self.**

For Pai, Koro is both a positive and a negative animus figure. He tries to stop her from achieving her desires and reaching the next level of her development. He devalues her because she is female. But Pai loves her grandfather, and he also loves her. He passes on his deep passion for their heritage to Pai. He tells her stories of her ancestors and their culture. Pai learns from Koro when she spies on his sessions teaching the boys. She retrieves the whale tooth necklace because she wants to make her grandfather happy. Koro is the catalyst for many of Pai's actions. He enables her to obtain what she desires. Pai's grandmother, Nanny Flowers, fits the role of shadow. She is the same sex as Pai, but has a wisdom and clarity that Pai does not yet possess. She does not agree with Koro's resentment of Pai's femaleness, but she understands it. Nanny Flowers is the opposite of Pai in both personality and self-image. She accepts her role as a female, but she picks her battles. Pai's grandmother leads her to her uncle for training and decides the best time to tell Koro that Pai found the necklace. She defends Pai and holds the family together. She guides Pai and gives her the advice and support that allow Pai to continue trying to fulfill her desires. Nanny Flowers knows how to be a strong woman without alienating the men in her life. Nanny Flowers, unlike Pai, is at peace with her identity. Nanny Flowers has the qualities that Pai lacks. By the end of the film, Pai gains the qualities that her grandmother has, and Pai is able to lead her people. The whale represents the self for Pai. The whale is the helpful animal that represents Pai's inner guiding factor. The whale that Pai rides is the leader of the other whales. Koro and the village use all of their strength to get the whale back into the water, stating that if the whale moves to the water, the other whales will follow. The fate of all of the beached whales depends on the leader whale. This is very much like the way the fate of Pai's people depends on Pai. When Pai rides the whale into the water, the whale enables her to become the leader of her people.

32. The Wizard of Oz

Film Data

Year: 1939

Director: Victor Fleming

Length: 101 minutes

Rated: N/A

Characters/Actors

Judy Garland:	Dorothy Gale
Frank Morgan:	Professor Marvel/The Wizard of Oz/The Gatekeeper/The Carriage Driver/The Guard
Ray Bolger:	Hunk/The Scarecrow
Bert Lahr:	Zeke/The Cowardly Lion
Jack Haley:	Hickory/The Tin Man
Billie Burke:	Glinda
Margaret Hamilton:	Miss Gulch/The Wicked Witch of the West
Clara Blandick:	Auntie Em

Connection to Chapters

Chapter 36. Applying Theory: A Proppian Analysis of *The Wizard of Oz*

Recommended Scenes

The opening scene of Dorothy discussing her problems, singing, and battling Miss Gulch occurs at 00:02:49 through 00:10:44.

The scene of the tornado occurs at 00:15:52 through 00:19:11.

The scenes in Oz occur from 00:19:30 through 01:39:12.

The scene of Dorothy encountering Glinda and The Wicked Witch occurs at 00:21:32 though 00:31:04.

The scene of Dorothy meeting the Scarecrow, Tin Man, and Lion occurs at 00:34:14 through 00:53:10.

The scene of the final battle with the Wicked Witch and her eventual destruction occurs at 01:15:45 through 01:27:13.

The scene Dorothy exposing the Wizard occurs at 01:28:24.

The scenes in Kansas resolving the story occur from 01:39:12 through the end of the film.

Instructor Viewing Information

The Wizard of Oz is a well-known musical featuring black-and-white and color scenes. Students should be familiar with the film, or at least the characters in the film. Adults will appreciate the musical numbers, humorous dialogue, and vibrant sequences. The film provides an enjoyable and interesting way to discuss rationalization of myths, changing audiences, and gender roles in myth. Those familiar with *The Wizard of Oz* as children will be able to examine the film with new insights and appreciation. *The Wizard of Oz* also provides a good way to introduce Proppian analysis.

Synopsis

Dorothy (Garland) lives on a Kansas farm with her Aunt Em (Blandick), Uncle Henry (Grapewin), and farm hands Hunk (Bolger), Zeke (Lahr), and Hickory (Haley). After mean Miss Gulch (Hamilton) takes away Dorothy's dog Toto, Toto escapes and Dorothy and Toto run away together. An encounter with traveling performer Professor Marvel (Morgan) convinces Dorothy to return home, but by then a tornado has hit the farm. Dorothy is knocked down by a broken window and collapses on her bed. When Dorothy awakens, she believes her house is being carried away by a tornado. She finds herself in the magical Land of Oz, where her house has flattened a witch with ruby slippers. She encounters good witch Glinda (Burke) and The Wicked Witch of the West (Hamilton). Dorothy spends her time in Oz trying to find a way to return home. Glinda gives Dorothy the magic ruby slippers and advises her to see the Wizard of Oz (Morgan). Dorothy is joined on her journey by the Scarecrow (Bolger) seeking a brain, the Tin man (Haley) seeking a heart, and the Lion (Lahr) seeking courage. Dorothy accidentally kills The Wicked Witch and then exposes the wizard as a well-intentioned fraud. The Wizard grants the requests of the group, but Dorothy needs the help of Glinda to return home. Glinda shows

Dorothy that she always had the power to return home. When Dorothy opens her eyes, she is back in Kansas, surrounded by her aunt, uncle, and the three farm hands. Dorothy is told she had a dream, but she believes it was real. At the end of the film, Dorothy finds the most important part of her experience was her appreciation for home.

Discussion Questions

1. **Explain how the film reflects concern for gender equality.**

   The most powerful characters in *The Wizard of Oz,* including the agents for good and evil, are women. Although the title of the film refers to the Wizard, it is Dorothy who is the film's main character. It is Dorothy's dreams and desires that are the focus of the film. At the start of the film, Dorothy shows her strength and bravery by standing up to Miss Gulch. When in Oz, Dorothy continues to be brave and to stand up for what she believes is right. When Dorothy, the Scarecrow, and the Tin Man encounter the Lion, it is Dorothy who refuses to cower in fear. Dorothy even hits the Lion for scaring the others. It is clear that Dorothy is the leader of the foursome, and her male companions in Oz look to her for guidance. She also faces the Wizard and Wicked Witch with bravery. In Oz, the two most powerful forces for good and evil are the two female witches. In Kansas, the most powerful characters are also female. Dorothy's nemesis in Kansas is Miss Gulch, the parallel character of The Wicked Witch. This point is emphasized by having the same actress play both parts. While Dorothy loves both her aunt and uncle, it is Aunt Em who Dorothy worries about and wants to see again. For Dorothy, Aunt Em represents home.

2. **Describe how the filmmakers used the rationalization process to make the film acceptable for adult audiences.**

   The film's opening sequences in Kansas show that Dorothy has the kind of realistic problems adults can understand. A mean but powerful resident of the town complains about Dorothy's dog Toto and uses local officials to try to take Toto from Dorothy. Dorothy's aunt and uncle are too busy with their own lives to help her. The farm hands are also busy and offer Dorothy philosophical advice that is not helpful. Dorothy feels dismissed and ignored and longs for a better place. She voices this desire when she sings "Somewhere Over the Rainbow." The bleak Kansas scenes are in black-and-white. In these scenes, the audience meets all of the real characters whose magical counterparts Dorothy meets in Oz. When a frightening tornado injures Dorothy, she either dreams or is transported to Oz. The adults in the audience can accept a vivid dream, while the children do not need the fantastic elements explained. The use of vibrant Technicolor for the Oz scenes supports the idea that Dorothy's adventures in Oz are a dream and a way of working out her problems in Kansas. But the Technicolor scenes also emphasize the magical elements of the story. When Dorothy awakens from her dream, she is in Kansas and the film returns to black-and-white. She recognizes the farmhands as characters in Oz, and the adults around her tell her she had a dream. Adult audiences accept Dorothy's adventures in Oz as a dream, which allows them to appreciate the fantastic elements of Oz.

3. **Explain how the film's incomplete ending is consistent with the idea that the overall effect is more important than resolving every problem in the tale.**

At the start of the film, Dorothy felt that her needs were dismissed and ignored on the farm. She also had the immediate problem of protecting Toto from Miss Gulch. While the situation with Toto is never resolved, Toto is with Dorothy at the end of the film. At the end of the film, Dorothy's aunt, uncle, the farmhands, and Professor Marvel surround Dorothy's bed. They are all glad to see her, and she sees they were all worried about her. As she tells them about her experiences in Oz, they tell her it was a dream. But they all listen. When Dorothy asks that someone believe her that Oz is real, Dorothy's uncle says he does believe her. Dorothy's family and the farmhands listen to her and show that they take her feelings seriously. She no longer feels ignored. Perhaps they will now also help her keep Toto. Dorothy no longer yearns for a better place. Dorothy makes this clear when she says the she knows that there is no place like home.

33. The X-Files, "The Erlenmeyer Flask"

Film Data

Year: 1994, Season 1, episode 23

Director: R. W. Goodwin

Length: 45 minutes

Rated: TV/14

Characters/Actors

David Duchovny: Fox Mulder

Gillian Anderson: Dana Scully

Lindsey Ginter: Crew Cut Man

Anne De Salvo: Dr. Anne Carpenter (as Anne DeSalvo)

Simon Webb: Dr. William Secare

Ken Kramer: Dr. Terrance Allen Berube

Jerry Hardin: Deep Throat

Connection to Chapters

Chapter 34. Applying Theory: How to Perform a Jungian Analysis

Chapter 41. *Stagecoach* and *Firefly:* The Journey into the Unknown in Westerns and Science Fiction

Recommended Scenes

The scene of Mulder and Deep Throat arguing about trust occurs at 00:11:02.

The scene of Mulder discovering the lab with tanks of people underwater occurs at 00:22:30.

The scene of Scully finding out about the extraterrestrial DNA occurs at 00:25:01.

The scene of Scully telling Mulder that she always held science sacred occurs at 00:27:25.

The scene of Deep Throat explaining the details of the experiment to Mulder and Scully occurs at 00:28:10 through 00:31:02.

The scene of the exchange, Deep Throat being shot, and the resolution of the story occurs at 00:41:48 through the end of the episode.

Instructor Viewing Information

The X-Files ran for nine seasons on television, from 1993 through 2002. FBI agents Fox Mulder (Duchovny) and Dana Scully (Anderson) investigate unsolved cases that may involve paranormal activity. "The Erlenmeyer Flask" is the last episode of the first season. Students may be familiar with the characters and series, but even those who are not should understand and enjoy this episode. Students should be cautioned about the complexities involved with applying Jungian analysis to popular entertainment like *The X-Files*. Some films and television programs that appear to be less serious works may seem to contain obvious archetypes. However, care must be taken to include the dark and humorous aspects of the characters and their relationships. In the case of Mulder and Scully, the characters are heroes, but the noir perspective of the story both supports heroic actions and undercuts them by representing the world as a hopeless kind of place in which a happy ending and personal fulfillment are not possible. *The X-Files* provides a good way to discuss how science, technology, government, and the individual are viewed in our current society. This episode also provides a good illustration of how popular entertainment reflects the concerns of its audience.

Synopsis

Agent Mulder gets a tip from his source, Deep Throat (Hardin), to investigate a police chase shown on a television news report. Mulder and Scully find a scientist, Dr. Terrance Allen Berube (Kramer), who is doing experiments on animals. The scientist ends up dead, and Mulder and Scully find that he was experimenting with extraterrestrial DNA. One of the subjects, Dr. William Secare (Webb), can now breathe underwater. He is also murdered. Eventually Mulder and Scully find a lab full of tanks with human beings breathing underwater. Deep Throat tells them that this is part of a secret government project. When Mulder is kidnapped, probably by government agents, Deep Throat brokers a deal for Mulder's release. Scully retrieves a flask containing what looks to be a hybrid human fetus and reluctantly gives it to Deep Throat to exchange for Mulder. During the exchange, an injured Mulder is returned and Deep Throat is shot. The episode ends with a recovered Mulder telling Scully that they have been reassigned, but he will continue searching for the truth. The final shot of the episode shows a jar containing the hybrid life form being placed in a file on the shelf of a room in the Pentagon.

Discussion Questions

1. **Explain how the episode shows the series' underlying assumptions about science and technology.**

   The X-Files clearly views science (particularly biology) and technology with suspicion. Scully and Mulder learn that Dr. Berube, the scientist they are investigating, was one of many involved in the Human Genome Project. But Dr. Berube was also involved in a much less respectable project. Scully and Mulder discover a government experiment using cloned bacteria and DNA that may be extraterrestrial. Mulder discovers humans being kept in tanks and breathing underwater. They also learn that the volunteers for this experiment were people with terminal diseases. But any sympathy for this situation is undercut by the heartless behavior of those in charge. While Dr. Berube was trying to help his dying friend, those in charge murder Dr. Berube and his friend. They also destroy the humans in the lab, supporting the idea that keeping the experiment a secret is more important than human life. Although Mulder's Deep Throat contact briefly alludes to the benefits of extraterrestrial gene therapy, the point of view of the episode makes it clear that the abuses of such research far outweigh any potential benefits. Even Scully, a doctor, tells Mulder that she always viewed science as something sacred, but now she does not know what to think. Humor is also used to emphasize the way technology is viewed with suspicion. When Mulder is captured, his captor points out that Mulder's cell phone has been ringing incessantly. When a tied up and beaten Mulder suggests that his captor answer it, his captor states that he does not like talking on the phone because he has a "thing about unsecured lines."

2. **Describe how the episode reflects the concerns of the audience about government and the military.**

   The very premise of the series views the government and military as corrupt and suspect. Although Mulder and Scully are FBI agents, they work with little support and much interference. Mulder receives his tips from an informant who seems to work for the government, but will not reveal the name of his job. When Mulder discovers the secret lab, his informant, Deep Throat, explains that this gene research was part of a top secret government project. He explains that the government was only interested in the science and technology of the research. When the experiments began to work, the government began to kill those involved. This reinforces the idea that government is corrupt and immoral, and does not value individual life. When Scully retrieves the flask containing human life, she must go to a secure government facility. She even guesses that the password is "purity control," which suggests a Nazi philosophy and science. Near the end of the episode Mulder calls Scully to tell her that the FBI is shutting their section down and that Mulder and Scully will be reassigned. Mulder says that order came from the top of the executive branch. The implication is that the corruption of the government exists at the very top levels. The final scene in the episode shows a secure file room in the Pentagon. A man in a suit places a jar with the hybrid life in a cardboard file on a shelf. A long shot shows a big room filled with many shelves of cardboard files.

3. **Explain how the characters in the episode view the importance of the individual over the group.**

While Scully and Mulder are partners, she often questions the importance of their investigation, while he is the one to keep pushing. They are at odds over the existence of extraterrestrials, although she continues to help him. Scully and Mulder are helped with cryptic hints from Deep Throat, but Mulder also views him with suspicion. When Deep Throat arranges to exchange the flask Scully took from the lab for Mulder, Scully is reluctant to give Deep Throat the flask. She tells him that she does not trust him because she knows nothing about him. He answers that she has no one else to trust. Here, the individual can only really trust himself or herself, and when others need to be trusted, trust is given with great reluctance. When Scully questions saving Mulder's life over so many others, Deep Throat explains that the discoveries Mulder and Fox made are just the beginning. He explains that Mulder and Scully are the only ones who can bring the evils to light. Here, the fate of all rests on two individuals. It is these individuals who can accomplish what no group can. The groups are corrupt and the individuals must rely on themselves. By the end of the episode, Deep Throat has been shot. With his dying breath he tells Scully, "Trust no one." Of course, this statement is shown in each episode. When Mulder tells Scully that they have been reassigned, he tells Scully that he will not give up. He explains that he cannot give up as long as the truth is out there. Here, it is up to the determination of one person to save all from the evil of the group.